FREEDOM IN CHRIST

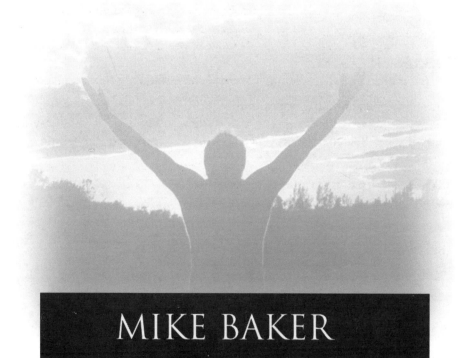

MIKE BAKER

HEARTSPRING PUBLISHING · JOPLIN, MISSOURI

Copyright © 2006
HeartSpring Publishing
www.heartspringpublishing.com
A division of College Press Publishing Co.

Toll-free order line 800-289-3300
On the web at www.collegepress.com

The 3:16 Series (Colossians 3:16)
"Let the word of Christ dwell in you richly . . . ."

Cover design by Brett Lyerla
Interior design by Dan Rees

Library of Congress Cataloging-in-Publication Data

Baker, Mike, 1965 Feb. 1–
    Freedom in Christ / by Mike Baker.
        p. cm. — (The 3:16 series)
    ISBN 0-89900-299-4 (softback)
    1. Bible. N.T. Galatians—Criticism, interpretation, etc.   2. Liberty—Religious aspects—Christianity—Biblical teaching.   I. Title.
    BS2685.6.F7B35 2005
    227'.406—dc22

                                                            2005030151

HEARTSPRING'S 3:16 SERIES

The Apostle Paul encouraged Christians in the first century and therefore us today to **"allow the Word of Christ to dwell in us richly"** (Colossians 3:16, *NIV*).

The 3:16 Series is based on this verse in Colossians. The series is designed primarily for small group study and interaction but will also prove fruitful for individual study. Each participant is encouraged to read the chapter before the group's meeting. The interaction questions are designed to be the focal point of your group's discussion time.

Psalm 119:11 says, *"I have hidden Your Word in my heart that I might not sin against You."* One noteworthy feature of this series is that each study includes a suggested memory verse (a short verse or two from the passage that is being studied). A sheet of these has been included at the back of the book for you to take these verses with you wherever you go and refer to them throughout your day.

The HeartSpring Publishing website will continually be updated with small group ideas and tips to further enhance your study of each New Testament book in the 3:16 series. Be sure to log on to www.heartspringpublishing.com (College Press) frequently!

> "Let the Word of Christ . . . have the run of the house.
> Give it plenty of room in your lives."
> (Col. 3:16 *The Message*)

PREVIEWING OUR STUDY OF GALATIANS

MIKE BAKER

Freedom. Let that word sink in. It is a powerful word and a powerful idea. Throughout history when people are oppressed, they seek freedom. When people are enslaved, they fight for freedom. When people are invaded and conquered, the idea of freedom prevents them from truly being controlled. During the years of slavery in America, the famous "Underground Railroad" was the dangerous path to freedom. In spite of possible punishment, torture, and even death, slave after slave risked everything to find freedom by escaping to the North. Why? Because freedom is a deep cry of the human heart. When someone is enslaved, he will make every attempt at setting himself free. But what happens when the best attempts at freedom result in the same unchanging condition? What happens when those who are enslaved are unable to free themselves?

The book of Galatians is about freedom for those who couldn't gain freedom on their own. Not freedom from physical oppression, but spiritual freedom from sin and its resulting slavery. The apostle Paul begins this letter as usual with greetings and blessings, but he wastes little time getting right to the point: "I am astonished that you are so quickly deserting the one who called you by the grace of Christ and are turning to a different gospel." He wants the Galatian believers to know that from his viewpoint they are making the unbelievable run from freedom back to slavery.

This teaching about freedom in Christ is just as important now as it was when it was written nearly twenty centuries ago. Astonishingly, many Christians today prefer the shackles of customs, traditions, rituals, and rules and flee the freedom of grace, faith, and the Holy Spirit. Why? A study of Galatians may help us find out, but before we begin, let's look briefly at the people who first received this letter.

The book we know as Galatians is believed by most biblical scholars to be the earliest Christian writing. Many believe this epistle to have been written in A.D. 49 (less than twenty years after the day of Pentecost and the beginning of the church as recorded in Acts 2). This letter is distinctive from Paul's other writings in that it is written to believers living in an entire region instead of addressing a person or a church in a specific city. This would be like writing a letter to the churches of Illinois instead of writing to First Church of Chicago. The region of Galatia would have included churches from Pisidian Antioch (there were two "Antiochs" in the New Testament world—one here in the region of Galatia and the other in Syria, from which Paul and Barnabas had been sent), Iconium, Lystra, and Derbe. From the first writing, we see that Paul understood that these letters would be passed from church to church and used for instruction. Indeed, he knew that as the Holy Spirit worked through him, he was in fact writing Scripture.

Paul had ministered extensively in these towns on his first missionary effort with Barnabas. You can find the details in Acts 13 and 14. In Antioch, Paul gave such a rousing sermon that the following week nearly the whole city gathered to hear the good news of Jesus (Acts 13:44). In Iconium, they spoke effectively again, but some opposition forced them to the cities of Lystra and Derbe. In Lystra, Paul and Barnabas experienced the highs and lows of ministry in one day. Upon entering the city, they healed a blind man and were worshiped as gods, but when some people from Iconium heard about the uproar they came and turned the people against Paul and Barnabas. By the end of the day, the crowd had stoned Paul and left him for dead. The next day he was preaching in Derbe.

In the end of Acts 14 we learn that while heading back to Antioch (Syria), Paul and Barnabas made a concerted effort to visit each of these new Galatian churches. In each city they reiterated the gospel message, appointed elders, and taught doctrine. Now, only two years later, Paul pens the book we know as Galatians. In it he encouraged these believers to remain in the freedom they had believed but were now walking away from. Throughout the book of Galatians, Paul delivered to the church then a resounding freedom message.

The message of freedom in Galatians rings true to the 21st-century ear like it did two millennia ago in the congregations at Antioch, Iconium, Lystra, and Derbe. But for us to understand it completely, we need to understand the issues of first-century Galatia and its culture. Mainly, three forces were at work in Galatia which impacted the influence of the church in that region: Judaizers (keepers of the Mosaic law and tradition), the Roman Empire (pagan culture), and Christianity (a rapidly growing sect called "The Way").

We know that the cities of Galatia had Jewish communities, because that is where Paul's preaching often took place. As a matter of fact, when Paul entered the city of Iconium in Acts 14, we are told they went to the Jewish synagogue "as usual." Jewish regulations required 10 Jewish men to be in residence in a city before a synagogue could be established. Obviously, each of these cities had a Jewish population, and this setting would be a natural place for Paul to begin his preaching. Being a Jew himself, he had an understanding of the law and traditions of faith which enabled him to introduce the message of Christ. Many of these Jewish people became the early believers in each of these cities, but Judaizers were Jews of a different kind.

The Judaizers were Jews by faith and race who were watchdogs for the Jewish faith. They believed that one could not be a part of God's kingdom without strict adherence to the Old Testament laws as handed down by Moses. Their issues were circumcision, yearly feasts, and ritualistic worship. Some of these defenders of the old covenant went to extraordinary lengths to stamp out the Christian movement that proclaimed freedom from these things. Paul himself was once a zealous persecutor of Christians in Jerusalem and Judea. He reminds his brothers and sisters that he "intensely persecuted the church" (Gal 1:13), "tried to destroy it" (Gal 1:13), and "was extremely zealous for the traditions of my fathers" (Gal 1:14). You may recall that it was on an anti-Christian mission to Damascus where Jesus confronted him about his persecution. The apostle knew all too well who he was dealing with. The passion, venom, and energy of this opposition movement within the Galatian churches was once his own.

Paul gave warning that these preachers of another gospel "which is really no gospel at all" (Gal 1:7) led to slavery and not freedom. He reserved some of his harshest words for these opponents of the freedom gospel: "let him be eternally condemned!" (Gal 1:9) and "as for these agitators, I wish they would go the whole way and emasculate themselves" (Gal 5:12). Why so brutal? The apostle saw this false preaching as something that would lead his brothers and sisters into slavery again. He says in Galatians 5:1, "Do not let yourselves be burdened again by a yoke of slavery."

Previewing Our Study of Galatians

Another influence in the Galatian church had to do with its location. It was in fact a part of the Roman Empire. As a territory of Rome, the majority of the general populace in these cities would have espoused Greek philosophy, lived a hedonistic lifestyle, and practiced a polytheistic faith. This is the pagan force that the apostles confronted as they came into town with their freedom message. Much like present-day America, the people of this "enlightened" culture would have claimed the freedom to rely on the human mind for truth and human experience for pleasure. Their tolerant view of the spiritual would have led them to claim all beliefs were valid. They revered philosophers, honored sports heroes, and idolized entertainers. The religion of Galatia was a combination of temple ritual and sexual expression. It sounds like people living freely, but Paul painted a more accurate picture of the slavery by which this culture was bound.

The apostle described life in both first-century Galatia and 21st-century America when he wrote, "The acts of the sinful nature are obvious: sexual immorality, impurity and debauchery; idolatry and witchcraft; hatred, discord, jealousy, fits of rage, selfish ambition, dissensions, factions, and envy; drunkenness, orgies and the like" (Gal 5:19-21). In Paul's mind, this "obvious" state of mankind was nothing more than slavery: "But the Scripture declares that the whole world is a prisoner of sin" (Gal 3:22).

This brings us to the third prevalent force in Galatia. True apostolic Christianity had made its own mark. Paul and Barnabas (along with their ever-increasing entourage) had truly impacted this region. Along with the persecutors of faith, there were people of faith. There were established congregations (probably more like house churches than what we experience today), anointed elder/leaders, and followers of Christ. Paul and Barnabas were certainly influencers and well known. The gift of healing and passion of preaching have a way of getting people's attention! In truth, the proponents of pagan culture and Jewish tradition were roused to defend themselves because Christianity had so thoroughly impacted Galatia.

Of course, this was the only truly freeing influence on this or any culture. Christianity taught freedom from religious ritual and sinful lifestyle. Paul would say, "It is for freedom that Christ has set us free" (Gal 5:1). He pled with them, "How is it that you are turning back to those weak and miserable principles? Do you wish to be enslaved by them all over again?" (Gal 4:9). This is the message of Galatians that we will examine over the next eleven chapters. Will we choose the slavery of religious practice or sin? Or will we choose the freedom that can only be found in Jesus?

Previewing Our Study of Galatians

The goal of this book is to encourage you and your group to choose freedom as we study the freedom message in the book of Galatians. In the church, both then and now, let freedom ring!

Chapter One: Freedom Gospel (Galatians 1:6-9)

Our study begins with a contrast between good news and bad news. The word "gospel" used in chapter one is a Bible word that literally translated means, "good news." Paul explains that there is the "good news" and there is bad "good news" (which is not really good news at all). In this chapter we will compare the two messages the Galatians were receiving and how these two messages sometimes enter today's church. Paul's message was the good news of grace through Jesus. His assertion is that any other message leads to eternal condemnation.

Chapter Two: Freedom for ALL (Galatians 2:1-10)

Until the beginning of the church, God's salvation message was a message primarily given to and through descendants of Abraham. It was a strictly Jewish message. Christ's audience, all of Jesus' disciples, and most of the original Jerusalem church were Jews. In this lesson we will learn that God had specifically called Paul to preach this gospel to the Gentiles (non-Jews). This means that freedom rings true not only for those connected to Christ by lineage, but to everyone regardless of race, heritage, or background.

Chapter Three: Freedom's Price (Galatians 2:20 & 21)

Freedom is very expensive. When a nation or a people live in freedom, it has been borne on the backs of young and weary soldiers in the midst of cold, lonely, and nasty battles and has cost the ultimate price: people's blood and lives. Basic life freedoms that many of us take for granted come as a result of someone else literally laying their life on the line. In the same way, our spiritual freedom from sin and death come at a price. In this lesson we will examine the incredible price that Jesus paid so that you and I could be free in him.

Chapter Four: Freedom through Faith (Galatians 3:1-14)

The pressing question for a slave is, "How can I become free?" In this section, Paul reminds his brothers and sisters that freedom comes from faith, not by observing rules. He uses Abraham as the prime example of a guy who was free, not because he did righteous acts but because he believed in God. He was free to be righteous because he believed in God. We will learn that we are blessed along with Abraham because of our faith. The common thread between the Christian and this man of faith is belief, not righteousness, yet righteousness will result because of our belief. Faith frees us to be righteous.

Chapter Five: Freedom and the Law (Galatians 3:19-25)

In this study we will address the purpose of the Old Testament Law. "Why do we even have the Old Testament?" many have been tempted to ask. Paul would say that even though the Law could in no way free us, it was a very important part of the freedom process. The Law was a guide for righteous living, it was a part of the story of promise, and it pointed to something better (Jesus). It was not Paul's intention to condemn the Law, but to see it in its proper place. We will learn that while following the Law will never bring freedom, understanding the law will lead us to the freedom message.

Chapter Six: Freedom by Relationship (Galatians 3:26-29/4:21-31)

In this chapter we learn that we find freedom by belonging to the family of God through relationship with Christ. Paul illustrates through the life of Abraham. His son Ishmael was not the son of the promise and lived a life of slavery. His son Isaac was the son of the promise and therefore heir to all of the promises God had made to his father. By living lives of faith, we become relatives of Abraham (children of the free woman) and by this relationship enjoy the freedom that comes with family privilege.

Chapter Seven: Freedom Opponents (Galatians 4:8-18)

For whatever reason, there are always those opposed to freedom. They actually fight against freedom. The Judaizers in the Galatian church filled this role. In this chapter we will ask three questions to reveal freedom's opponents: Are you giving a list of rules or offering a relationship? Does your message bring joy or take it away? Are you keeping people out or inviting them in? There are those whose message about God is an invitation to rules, drudgery, and exclusivity. This is not a freedom message!

Chapter Eight: A Freedom Picture (Galatians 5:1-12)

In this chapter Paul gets very practical about what freedom looks like in everyday life. We will study his humorous use of the word "cut" and his passion against his adversaries. But we will focus on a life of freedom that stands firm, eagerly anticipates the future, and doesn't allow something or someone else to cut in on the race we are running.

Previewing Our Study of Galatians

Chapter Nine: Freedom by the Spirit (Galatians 5:16-26)

On this road to freedom, God has equipped us with his very presence to influence us. This teaching contrasts two different masters to which people may submit. Either we submit to the sinful nature and the results will be death and exclusion from the Kingdom of God, or we submit to the Spirit and exhibit the fruit of a Spirit-filled life. Of course, it is a life of love, joy, peace, patience, kindness, goodness, faithfulness, gentleness, and self-control that leads to real freedom.

Chapter Ten: Freedom to Serve (Galatians 6:1-10)

Service is the expression of freedom. When people are truly free, they are able to notice the needs of those around them. People who are captive focus only on themselves, but those who are free are able to notice and meet the needs of others. This portion of our teaching will guide us to serve those struggling with the restraints of sin, lighten the load of other people's problems, and authentically serve with humility. We will learn that a life spent sowing seeds of servanthood will reap an eternal, spiritual harvest.

Chapter Eleven: Freedom's Symbol (Galatians 6:11-18)

In an incredible paradox, Paul closes his teaching on freedom by pointing us to its ultimate symbol. Even though the cross was the final chapter in many prisoners' lives, it represents freedom to the Christian. Only in embracing the cross will we find true freedom. We will be encouraged not to avoid the cross, but to take pride in the cross and to let the cross mark our lives. In so doing, we will hear freedom's ring throughout history from the most important event of all time—God dying for man.

Previewing Our Study of Galatians

TABLE OF CONTENTS

FREEDOM IN CHRIST

CHAPTER ONE

FREEDOM GOSPEL

GALATIANS 1:6-9

I saw it on one of those never-ending plane flights home. Maybe you've had a similar experience. You're three hours late, the air traffic is so heavy that you have circled the airport three times, and the pretzels have had no effect on your growling stomach. In one of these moments a few years back, I instinctively reached for the in-flight magazine (which I had already read three times). After thumbing through some travel reviews, my eyes caught an advertisement for free sunglasses. I know the adage, "If it's too good to be true, it usually is." But on this occasion, I thought, "What can it hurt to call?" I ripped the page from the magazine and slipped it into my briefcase.

The next day, having recovered from my travels, I went through my bag and retrieved the advertisement. I read it again, and sure enough, the sunglasses were still free. I promptly picked up the phone and dialed the 800 number in anticipation. The pleasant and informative receptionist asked me a series of questions about the specific sunglasses I was interested in. I told her what style I wanted. I picked out the color. I told her where I had seen the ad. "Hah!" I thought, "My wife is wrong, these sunglasses really are free." This kind lady continued, "Would you be interested in a stylish strap to go with your purchase?" She asked if I would be interested in the special cleaning cloth and solution. "How about a special carrying case?" Finally, she offered, "For $7.95 we can have these wonderful sunglasses to you in two days." In a matter of minutes my state of the art, latest fashion sunglasses were on the way. And what exactly, was the cost of these "free" glasses? Twenty-nine dollars.

Sometimes free isn't free.

If the apostle Paul were writing a letter to me about sunglasses, he would say, "I am astonished that you are paying $29.00 for free sunglasses." He would contend that "free" must by definition mean a gift at no cost to the person who receives it. In fact he would say that "free sunglasses" are good news. But the good news of free sunglasses that cost $29.00 is not good news at all. This is the point Paul wants us to see.

> **Sometimes free isn't free.**

The Definition of "Good News"

There were two forms of "good news" being circulated in the Galatian churches. Both proposed that there was some good news regarding God. Notice that Paul's message and the message of the Judaizers both claimed that someone could have relationship with God, and that is good news. Paul's message was truly good news because this holy relationship was based on a free gift. Contrast this with the opposing message that the good news of an eternal relationship must be earned by the recipient. In this chapter we will examine these two "good news" messages, but first let's define "good news."

The word "gospel" must be the focus of our discussion, for Paul uses it five times in the four verses we are studying in this lesson. "Gospel" seems like a church word. It is always paired with such religious sounding words. A gospel choir is obviously a bunch of people singing in a church. Gospel music is a collection of songs about God. A gospel message is a long talk by a smart guy who uses big words. The Gospel Hour is a television show that combines all of these things. Although the word "gospel" seems like something that would only belong in a church service, in the first century it was a common term.

Simply translated the word "gospel" means "good news." This Greek word has been transliterated as our English word "evangelism." In a day when there were no cell phones, e-mails, or live newscasts, news was often sent by designated messengers. The word "gospel" was specifically used to denote those messengers and messages that brought good or prosperous information. As a matter of fact, the word "angel" (messengers from God with good news) is a root word of this word gospel.

Virtually any declaration of some positive information could be gospel. "I just won the lottery"-gospel. "My son got a scholarship to

Hometown University"-gospel. "I'm getting married"-gospel. "I'm cancer free"-gospel. "Your mother is going to be all right"-gospel. "The war is over"-gospel. It just so happens that in Paul's mind the ultimate good news was that Jesus "gave himself for our sins to rescue us . . ." (Gal 1:3). Unfortunately, the Galatians were being drawn to another kind of gospel.

The "good news" hitting the Galatian airwaves was a form of religion that required ritual and form. This was not a new concept for the Galatian mind. As we have already mentioned, there was at least some Jewish influence in this region. The recipients of this letter from the apostle would have had at least an awareness of some of the corporate worship practices of their Jewish neighbors. They would have witnessed fasting, sacrifices on an altar, times of prayer, incense burning, and dietary practices during certain times of the year. Many may have even been familiar with some of the readings from the Old Testament Law.

Aside from witnessing Jewish religious practice, these people would have had an understanding of the pagan rituals that permeated their culture. First, there were numerous temples erected in honor of a variety of gods and goddesses in each city. Worship in these temples could include sacrifices (animal and agricultural), burning of incense, feasting, and ritualistic sex. Each maintained a system of priests and priestesses that would have been held in high esteem.

The good news of these religious forms was simple. The common Jewish message was, "If you follow God's laws, celebrate his feasts, sacrifice appropriately at his altar, and have the mark of circumcision, you will earn his love based on your obedience to him." The pagan message was similar. "If you appease the gods through sacrifice, celebrate man (indulge the passions), seek the higher knowledge, and pray for good fortune, it will be better for you in the afterlife."

Paul considered both the Jewish and pagan rituals a different gospel. It wasn't the message he preached when he was among them; it was a perversion of the gospel. The problem with the false gospel teachings was that Paul knew it had eternal implications. Maybe that's why he condemned anyone who preached anything other than the true gospel message. To make his point he repeated the warning twice in verses eight and nine: "may they be eternally condemned."

What Is the Meaning of "Free"?

Unfortunately, this gospel that isn't really "good news" is alive and well two millennia later, and it feeds on confusing rules and a desire most people have to please God. This can express itself in a number of man-made laws. Do some of these sound familiar?

"Christians shouldn't see R-rated movies." "People should dress up when they go to church (God deserves our best)." "It is wrong to drink alcohol of any kind." "A true believer will pray at least an hour a day." "Christian music should be quiet and meditative." "Christian parents should put their kids in Christian school." "Christians shouldn't play violent video games." "Christians shouldn't own guns." "We should be active in environmental issues." "A real Christian wouldn't drive an expensive car." "You shouldn't wear clothing from Abercrombie & Fitch." "It's wrong for a Christian to have tattoos." "Guys shouldn't pierce their ears (or nose, eyebrows, or anything else for that matter)." "Don't cuss." "You should be at the church building every time the doors are open." "You should give more to (insert cause here)." Confused yet?

"Religion" is made up of a bunch of "do's" and "don'ts" and it causes spiritual confusion and frustration. All of the above statements are okay in and of themselves. Perhaps they are even desirable, but they aren't part of the gospel message. They are perceptions or opinions—rules made by well-meaning people. But who do you listen to?

> **"Religion" causes spiritual confusion and frustration.**

Some really great Christian people drink beer and wine. Some believers use words that weren't bad in their upbringing, yet are offensive to others. Some brothers and sisters drive BMWs and Hummers. Some wear ties to church and others wear jeans and shorts.

As a result of these rules, the body of Christ becomes fragmented. One person is driven to find a bunch of people who believe exactly like he does in order to feel religious. This is why there are innumerable denominations in the world today. People are attracted to God, but they are confused by how they can get to him. In the end this variety of "God messages" doesn't lead to freedom. On the contrary it causes people to revert to the slavery of religion. They end up listening to the voice of man instead of God. Many people, both in and out of church, have heard so many things about God and how they should live that they are, in fact, slaves to religious rules and conditions. Worse yet, they reject this so-called freedom and choose to remain in slavery to sin.

We often spend our lives in this spiritual confusion, totally frustrated with who we are. We desire to follow the rules that will gain God's approval, yet we fail so often we are sure God can't be pleased. And on those rare occasions when we feel like we've got a grasp on this obedience toward God;

> **We spend much of our lives being religious yet lacking assurance that we are getting any closer to him.**

someone makes a new rule, or we learn of another faith form that we are not practicing. We spend much of our lives being religious yet lacking assurance that we are getting any closer to him.

This is not freedom. You know it. I know it. Paul reminds the Galatians that they are not living freely. What was the good news that Paul had originally preached to these early believers? He simply shared the true gospel of Jesus Christ. Let's look briefly at three parts of this good news as outlined in his opening greeting to these Christians.

The Real Good News Means Freedom

The first step to freedom is an understanding that Jesus willingly gave himself so that we could be free. This is the beginning of freedom. Every person who has or ever will live—every woman, man, boy, and girl—has sinned. That's bad news, because sin comes with a consequence—death. The good news that Paul declared to the Galatians and to people everywhere is that Jesus paid for those sins.

As a matter of fact, we have record of one of those sermons that Paul preached in the Galatian city of Antioch in the book of Acts. First of all, we know that on this particular day, almost the entire city gathered to hear Paul's words (see Acts 13:44). What was the message they had come to hear? Were they interested by some new religion? Was it a special set of rules that they had never heard of before that intrigued them? Did Paul and Barnabus have a new method for being disciplined and following the commandments? What made an entire city come to hear his message? It was the simplicity of some really good news. "I want you to know that through Jesus the forgiveness of sins is proclaimed to you" (Acts 13:38).

The good news then and now is that Jesus paid for every sin that humankind ever committed. This is the freedom message. Every lie told, every object stolen, every rule broken, every adulterous relationship, every murder, every harmful word, every false judgment, every drunken moment, every lustful thought, and every malicious motive is forgiven because Jesus gave himself for our sins! Words can't describe the spiritual relief this brings to us. There are not enough "I'm sorry's" in the world to make up for all we've done. There is no way we could fix all the messes we've made. We couldn't begin to cleanse the dirt from our hearts and enter into the holiness of God. But in one act—namely Jesus' death on a cross—everything was eternally fixed and we were set free.

> There are not enough "I'm sorry's" in the world to make up for all we've done.

We must understand clearly the message of the gospel here. There is absolutely nothing we could do to set ourselves free. Only because Jesus made the sacrifice can you and I be free.

Not only did Jesus save us from the slavery of sin; he also rescued us from the results of sin in this world. Paul says in verse three Jesus came to "rescue us from the present evil age." Rescue is a common theme of life. This may be why so many people declared the television classic *Gilligan's Island* an all-time favorite.

The premise of the show was that seven people were stranded on a desert island, and they learned to live together. They built homes. They found food and water sources. With the professor's help they were even able to re-create some conveniences. They were very resourceful. They worked together for the common good, and they were able to appreciate each other's differences. There were good relationships and fun and laughter. The setting wasn't that bad either. They lived in a tropic paradise with palm trees and beaches. But despite all of these positives, the theme of every show was centered on these castaways trying to get home. They needed someone to rescue them.

This world is our Gilligan's Island. We try to make it work. We survive relationships. We have some nice things. There are wonderful moments of joy and laughter with people. We get married and have children and grandchildren. We enjoy some comforts and experience some truly remarkable parts of God's creation. But there is something deep inside that desires more. When we consider the sin and corruption and hopelessness of our island, we want to be rescued.

The good news message is that we have been freed from the evil of this world and the influence that Satan has over it. We certainly would have been eternally grateful for God's forgiveness had that been the extent of the good news, but God not only freed us from sin through Jesus, he also freed us from this earth. He has another place for us.

The final piece of this good news is that this freedom message is the will of God. Paul concludes verse four with a very important phrase, "according to the will of our God and Father." Unlike the pagan gods who seemed a bit indifferent and even amused by the state of humanity, the eternal God in heaven initiated this path to freedom, and he will see it through. Even the Jewish perspective of God was that people must follow his laws strictly or else be rejected by him forever. The gospel is the exact opposite. God loves us forever regardless of what we do toward him. God's plan for freedom for mankind is solely dependent upon his will. He had the plan. He set it in motion. He gave his Son.

> The best news of all is not that we pursue God, but that he pursues us.

He paid our price. He is making us into what we were created to be. And he will bring all believers to an eternal home in glory. The best news of all is not that we pursue God, but that he pursues us.

It strikes me as I write these words that many readers will be incredibly uneasy with this whole concept. On some level, most of us want God to love us because we deserve it. Beyond that, we desire to somehow pay him back. This is human nature. But it is not a part of God's good news. You might as well become comfortable with two parts of the gospel. First of all, you don't deserve what God has done for you and no effort will ever make you worthy. Second, you can never pay God back for his incredible gift! You simply don't have the resources or time to repay the debt he paid for you.

This may be the most difficult of all theologies. Grace is about freedom and it is totally free. There is no reason to read another verse of the Bible unless we embrace this idea. This is why Paul wrote these words we have studied together. He is encouraging all Christians to stay with the freedom message. Freedom is good news. Running to other "good news" is like returning to slavery that you have been delivered from.

The final thought for this part of our study is that we should not listen to any other form of good news. According to the apostle, if some angel from heaven flew down and came to your house for supper and tried to convince you that there is another gospel of God; ignore the wings and halo and cover your ears. As a matter of fact, if Paul himself came to town and spoke at your church on Sunday morning and preached a different message than what they had previously preached; you shouldn't listen to him.

When Jesus came into the world, an angel appeared to some shepherds in a field and proclaimed, "I bring you good news . . . that will be for all the people" (Luke 2:10). The story of Christianity is still good news. It is still free and it still brings freedom. It is for all people. Don't desert it for anything else. 3:16

Living Free

1. As a group contact someone who is in jail or prison and adopt the prisoner as a pen pal. This will be a reminder to the group of the captivity that sin brings into our lives, and give a practical opportunity to participate in delivering the message of freedom to others.

2. Describe your life before Christ to the others in your small group. What was enslaving about your life then?

3. If you were to make some rules about God, what list might you come up with? Don't give church answers like, "the ten commandments." Be specific about how you think people should live for God.

4. When are you tempted to impose this list of beliefs on other people?

5. What rules did your church have growing up? What was your response both then and now? If you didn't grow up going to church, what was your impression of the rules? How did you respond to this impression?

I want you to know, brothers, that the gospel I preached is not something that man made up. ¹²I did not receive it from any man, nor was I taught it; rather, I received it by revelation from Jesus Christ.

CHAPTER TWO

FREEDOM FOR ALL

GALATIANS 2:1-10

Like most, I have spent much of my life trying to fit in. My first strong recollection of trying to belong is my freshman year of high school. When I was fourteen years old, a new brand of tennis shoe hit the market: Nike. The Nike phenomenon swept the nation. Back then we pronounced the word differently. (Nike rhymed with "bike," not "Mikey.") The pronunciation really didn't matter to me though. I just knew they were the coolest looking tennis shoes ever, and I had to have a pair.

There was only one problem. In a day when you could get a perfectly good pair of tennis shoes for $10–$15, Nikes were an outrageous $65! I begged my mom and dad for a pair, but down deep I knew my family couldn't afford tennis shoes that expensive, so I did the next best thing. I went to K-Mart and bought a pair of generic white high tops with the now-famous black swoosh curving down instead of up. In an attempt to fit in, I bought a cheap imitation and in the end wasn't any cooler for it. As a matter of fact, on the occasion that someone would notice the upside down swoosh, I had to endure the ridicule that only high school students can dish out. I failed at fitting in.

It's hard to be something that you are not. Another attempt at acceptance and fitting in came later in my adult life. By this time I was 30, I had several pairs of Nike tennis shoes, and I wished they were only $65! In this instance, a ministry friend of mine had asked me to come to his church in the south and spend three days doing youth ministry training and preaching for their Sunday morning service. I gladly accepted, but there was one condition on my coming. I had to change my name!

My friend explained that several years earlier this congregation had a minister who had stolen some money from the church and left under the worst of circumstances. It was a deep wound that had split the church and left many disillusioned and angry. You can probably guess that his name was Mike Baker. There is no way my friend could advertise a weekend of spiritual growth and ministry training with my name on it and hope to succeed. So for the entire weekend, I used my middle name. It was one of the most surreal experiences of my life. In order to be accepted in this congregation I had to be somebody that I wasn't. I vowed never to go by another name again.

In the last part of chapter two of Galatians we find the apostle Peter trying to fit in to two different groups. He has apparently come up to Antioch (in Syria) to hang out with the church there that Paul and Barnabas had established. He was Jewish by race and was one of the leading figures in the early church, but when he arrived in this Gentile region he began to socialize with these Gentile believers.

Apparently, he had been invited to several homes for a meal. Now it was against Jewish custom for a Jew to eat with a Gentile, but Peter apparently understood his freedom in Christ and accepted. We don't know exactly what happened. Maybe Peter threw off the phylacteries and had some bacon wraps. Maybe he ate without washing himself according to Jewish pre-meal tradition. Perhaps he radically skipped Saturday night service at the synagogue. Whatever the case, he apparently wasn't afraid to be a part of the Gentile Christian life. Unfortunately, when other leaders from the Jerusalem church came to town, he declined opportunities to socialize with his newfound Gentile friends, preferring the company of people of his own heritage. He acted as if it were wrong for Jews to socialize with Gentiles and resumed the Jewish custom of eating only with people of his own race. Even Paul's ministry partner Barnabas was caught up in this hypocrisy. This left the Gentile congregation puzzled and Paul righteously indignant. Paul realized Peter's position as a great church leader, but he knew he had to rebuke him for his lack of integrity.

Peter was experiencing an internal struggle between his Jewish heritage and his faith in Christ. In his mind he knew that non-Jews were equally welcome in the Kingdom of his Lord, but in his heart he wanted to retain the respect of his Jerusalem brothers. This struggle marked much of the debate of the early church and is part of the point Paul is trying to make about freedom and grace to the Galatian churches. In this section he answers the crucial question: Is the freedom of God's kingdom available to everyone?

In Galatians 2:1-10, Paul answers the question, "Is the freedom of God's kingdom available to everyone?" This seems like an amazing question to our 21st-century ears. Of course, everyone is welcome in the church. But a brief history of God's movement among the nation of Israel may give us an understanding of why early Jewish Christians balked at such a notion. You'll remember that God had chosen Abraham and his descendants to be the blessed people of God. You'll recall how God fought battles against and ordered the destruction of other nations and peoples. The greatest king, David, was promised the throne forever, and even in the midst of Israel's sin and God's apparent abandonment, the Jews sought a Messiah, an anointed ruler.

When Christ came, he was born to Jewish parents and raised according to Jewish customs. He learned, worshiped, and lived according to Jewish norms. When he began his ministry, it was primarily among Jewish people as he proclaimed the kingdom they had anticipated. When Jesus chose his most intimate friends and followers, they were of the same nationality. All of his teachings and indeed his very life were fulfillments of Jewish Scriptures. Christianity was born of the Jewish faith, nation, and people.

Of course, God was not anti-Gentile. Throughout the story of the Old Testament, he worked grace in people of many nationalities and races. He used foreign kings to accomplish his will. He worked salvation in the lives of many non-Jews. It's just that his plan of salvation was framed in the ancestry of Abraham and his descendants. Paul even says in his letter to the Romans, "What advantage, then, is there in being a Jew . . . ? Much in every way! First of all they have been entrusted with the very words of God" (Rom 3:1-2).

People of many races have taken it upon themselves to associate their heritage with God's favor. On a large scale this has resulted in wars fought on behalf of countries who believed God was on their side. On a local level, this has caused congregational bias towards a certain race, socioeconomic group, or physical appearance. Within congregations those who are "right" and "favored" by God because of their theology have caused fragmentation which leads to church splits. This part of the apostle's letter teaches us that this attitude couldn't be further from God's plan.

Let's personalize this even more. Few people in the church today would admit to having a prejudice toward a certain race or social level (even if they do so by their actions). However, many people who call themselves Christian would have a set of rules (self-devised, or taught, consciously or subconsciously) that exclude certain behaviors and therefore anyone who is attached to that behavior. Frequently, outsiders are led to believe that they have to become or do something to be a part of the kingdom of God; they have to change who they are to belong. But our spiritual instinct tells us that the kingdom of God is for all mankind and the Scripture confirms it. What does freedom for all really mean?

People of All Races

Paul had been doing ministry for fourteen years among the Gentiles when he returned to Jerusalem to report to the leaders there what God was doing. As a result of a vision, he made his way to the most important meeting in his life. For support he took his faithful ministry friend Barnabas and perhaps as an example, he took a Gentile convert named Titus.

As a person of Greek descent, Titus obviously wasn't circumcised and would provide living proof of the grace of God in the lives of non-Jews. It would not have been uncommon for Paul to insist that his Greek brother be circumcised before an audience with those "who seemed to be important," but he was convinced that circumcision had nothing to do with Christianity. So he brought Titus as he was. We should not assume that there was not some apprehension on the apostle's part. He was seeking approval from the unofficial governing body of the young church. They could have very well rejected him and his ministry. The result would have been that he had run in vain for fourteen years.

The verdict? The elders and leaders in the original church in Jerusalem realized that the gospel was open to all nations without exception. Paul uses an important phrase to describe how God looked at the "important" people in verse six. He teaches us a very important lesson about God when he says, "God does not judge by external appearance." God doesn't judge by external appearance regarding apostolic authority, and he doesn't dispense his grace according to race. The lesson here is that Titus (a Greek by birth) and Barnabas (a Jew) were both welcome to be a part of the church.

When it comes to racial attitudes in today's church, this part of Scripture should be clear to every Christian. It is the believer's responsibility to promote the gospel of freedom as a message for all people. Pastors and teachers should teach this truth and congregations should live it out. In this way, we can bring to earth what will be in heaven.

> It is the believer's responsibility to promote the gospel of freedom.

After this I looked and there before me was a great multitude that no one could count from every nation, tribe, people and language, standing before the throne and in front of the Lamb. They were wearing white robes and were holding palm branches in their hands. And they cried out in a loud voice: "Salvation belongs to our God, who sits on the throne, and to the Lamb" (Rev 7:9-10).

People of All Backgrounds

A close look at our study will reveal people from a variety of backgrounds. Of course there is Paul, whose background we have already mentioned. He was a member of the educated, spiritual elite—the son of a Pharisee. He knew the law and all of the prophecies about the Messiah, but it took a personal visit on a road trip to Damascus to truly see the Christ.

In verse nine we are given the names of three of the "pillars of the church." James was Jesus' biological half-brother. He and the rest of his family had struggled with belief early in Jesus' ministry. They even went at one point to "take charge of him, for they said, 'He is out of his mind'" (Mark 3:21). Apparently growing up in the same house with Jesus didn't necessarily lead to faith in him.

The other "pillars" didn't get to know Jesus until he was thirty years old. At the beginning of his ministry Jesus called two fishermen named Peter and John while they were on the job. Later Luke observed that they "were unschooled and ordinary men" (Acts 4:13). But even though they were ordinary, Jesus invested in them for three years to make them disciples who would become fishers of men.

Again, look at Titus. All we know of him from these verses is that he was Greek, which is enough to tell us that he was raised in a polytheistic society with a philosophic worldview, and that he might have had an advanced education.

These characters begin to paint for us a picture of a church made up of people from vastly different backgrounds and upbringings. The early church was made up of those who had been highly educated teachers and those who had been simple fishermen. It consisted of formerly pious leaders and previously hedonistic pagans. The background check on Christians is not a study in uniformity. We've all come from different places.

> The background check on Christians is not a study in uniformity.

In our particular congregation we have people who have no idea what a hymn is and some who were raised singing all seven stanzas.

We have those who came from a broken home and those who came from a "father knows best" home. There are those who were wild in high school and college and those who weren't. Some of our members grew up in extreme wealth and others grew up in the ghetto. Every Sunday, we have people in attendance who have served time and those who have served their country. The church is made up of people from all different backgrounds, and of course, this is the way it should be.

"Here there is no Greek or Jew, circumcised or uncircumcised, barbarian, Scythian, slave or free, but Christ is all, and is in all" (Col 3:11).

People of All Ministries

There is one final freedom we need to mention under the category of "all." Every day we see people from all backgrounds mesh to create the Body of Christ. This means that all of these different people from different backgrounds must be free to minister in a variety of ways. This is part of the freedom gospel.

Another look at verses 8-10 will reveal two distinct but equally valid ministries. Peter was called to minister among the Jews. He spent most of his teaching time building upon the teaching and laws of the Old Testament. He instructed Jews that Jesus was the fulfillment of the Law, the embodiment of Messianic prophecies, and the God of the patriarchs. Peter took his audience from old covenant to new, from law to grace, and from God's presence to his indwelling. The tabernacle, the history, and the promises illustrated Jesus' teachings. Peter no doubt celebrated the feasts and sang the Psalms. Paul, on the other hand, had a much different ministry.

Paul moved among people who debated and spoke philosophically about the meaning of life. He preached to people who worshiped many gods and had a high regard for learning. His ministry was contingent on learning the culture (sometimes different in each city) and teaching that God through Jesus was relevant. He used miracles to expand the Kingdom. He was beaten and jailed for such strange sounding ideas. Paul had to reason with his audience. He had to become "like one not having the law" and "all things to all men, so that by all possible means I might win some." (1 Cor 9:21-22). Notice the word "all." "All" men were important, so "all" means of winning someone to Jesus were appropriate. This formed the creative methodology of Paul's ministry to the Gentiles.

God blessed both of these ministries. Paul mentions in verse eight that God was at work in both ministries even though they were nearly opposite in their approach to sharing the gospel. This is the point for us. God uses a variety of callings, methods, and ideas to reach all kinds of people. Within his church we find amazing diversity in ministry.

> God uses a variety of callings, methods, and ideas to reach all kinds of people.

Throughout history the church has been notorious for not accepting other forms of ministry. The hippies of the group, Jesus People USA, were hardly welcomed into the church in the 1960s with their long hair, torn jeans, and message of peace. Billy Sunday didn't endear traditionalists with his street preaching laced with expletives during the 1920s. The band "Stryper" was marginalized by church leaders in the 1980s. The same songs that were criticized in the 1600s from the pen of Martin Luther set to tavern tunes, were held as sacred by those who opposed the "contemporary Christian music" movement of the 1990s.

Christians have a tendency to reject forms of ministry that they are either unfamiliar with or uncomfortable with. All of the above mentioned methods of sharing the freedom gospel were valid and effective, yet many in the church stood in judgment against them. There are some lessons for us to learn.

First, every Christian should have a ministry that he or she is passionate about which involves sharing the gospel. It may be an established ministry within your church, or one that God has laid on your heart. We may serve in the nursing home, in the local jail or prison, sports arenas, or in any number of places. The point is that God has called all of us to the task of preaching the gospel just like he had Peter to the Jews and Paul to the Gentiles.

Second, every Christian should refrain from judging whether or not another Christian's ministry is valid. We are called to serve not judge.

> We are called to serve not judge.

In a statement about judging the work of other apostles and leaders, the apostle would later write to the Corinthians, "who am I to judge another man's servant?" The point is that God is our master, and he will condemn or commend us according to his purpose.

Finally, the variety of styles, passions, gifts, and callings within the church is a display of God's incredible creativity. Christians should spend time celebrating how God uses each of us and our differences for his glory. The goal is not to become totally alike in Christ, it is to accept each others' differences so that he can make us one.

The result of this Jerusalem visit is the last item we must consider. Paul made his way to Jerusalem to present his case for ministry to the apostles and leaders there. Admittedly, there was some apprehension on his part (not to mention Titus's fear that they may require him to be circumcised!). But when it was all said and done, the elders in Jerusalem confirmed that the gospel is freedom for all: all races, all backgrounds, all ministries, and they sealed it with a handshake. We don't know what exactly the "right hand of fellowship" was, but we do know that it was a show of support, brotherhood, and camaraderie.

Maybe the church is meant to be more about shaking hands than pointing fingers. Perhaps there should be fewer fists in the air and more hands on the shoulder. This study may be a call to open up our arms instead of crossing them. If only the church would touch, clasp, and embrace; then maybe we could be the ones in a fragmented world to declare freedom for all. [3:16]

> **We need more shaking of hands and less pointing of fingers, more open arms and less crossed ones.**

Living Free

1. Have you ever felt left out, even within the church body? Reflect on a time you didn't "fit in." Answer this for both your local congregation and the church worldwide.

2. What kind of prejudices did you grow up with? (Hint: these are often taught by your parents.)

3. What has changed these views over time?

4. What kinds of people don't "fit in" with your church? Why?

5. What could you do as a small group to ensure people within your local church fit in more easily?

6. Have each member of your group share the spiritual background they came from?

7. If you thought no one would laugh and you could start any ministry you wanted; what would it be?

| Memory Verse Gal 2:7-8 | *On the contrary, they saw that I had been entrusted with the task of preaching the gospel to the Gentiles, just as Peter had been to the Jews. ⁸For God, who was at work in the ministry of Peter as an apostle to the Jews, was also at work in my ministry as an apostle to the Gentiles.* |

CHAPTER THREE

FREEDOM'S PRICE

GALATIANS 2:20 & 21

Perhaps the most famous war footage in American history was recorded in Normandy, France, at a place called Omaha Beach. On June 6, 1944, in a decisive World War II battle, American soldiers hit the shore and were greeted with enemy fire from the cliffs that rose above the sand. Defenseless, man after man was gunned down as they poured out of the boats to storm the German stronghold. They kept coming even as the carnage mounted; they were determined to reach their goal. By the day's end, they had broken through the enemy lines and had established the American position. But this victory was expensive!

The Cost

In footage now made famous by and reenacted in the movie *Saving Private Ryan*, those of us who weren't there are able to witness the devastation. The graphic images are now seared into our minds: body parts ripped off by machine-gun fire, literally strewn along the beach. The corpses of fallen soldiers wash in and out with the ebb and flow of each wave. The water takes on a ruddy hue, stained with blood. Those who survive the bloody onslaught wander around in shock looking for missing buddies. It is a historically tragic moment, and one that few Americans can relive without our emotions rising to the surface.

As tragic as this battle was, it was only part of the story of World War II. In all, American forces recorded 292,131 casualties from this bloody conflict. Death is part and parcel of war. However, this is not the only war American troops have participated in. The American Revolution cost 4,435 lives. The War of 1812 cost 2,260 lives. Fifty-three thousand soldiers died in World War I. The fighting in Korea surrendered over 33,000 lives, and another 47,000 were killed in Vietnam. And the result of all these deaths? In a word: freedom.

Every American who lives in a home of his choice is able to do so as a result of these deaths. Every time our government holds an election, American citizens have the privilege of voting, in part, because of these deaths. We have a president and not a king because soldiers died. We can speak our minds because someone else paid with his life. It is by the shed blood of literally thousands of soldiers throughout our history that gives us the right to work, live, and worship as free people.

> **Death is part and parcel of war.**

This brings us to the point of Galatians 2:20-21. The freedom we have in Christ comes at a price, and Paul was reminded of it every day.

In the most famous scene never recorded but dramatically re-created in many movies and paintings (the most recent being Mel Gibson's *The Passion*), a solitary figure is suspended between earth and sky on a hill called Golgotha. He and two criminals gasp for every breath as they endure a Roman crucifixion. As the midday sun darkens, the matted hair and blood streaked frame is barely recognizable as human. Soldiers feign worship and gamble beneath this torturous scene. One criminal curses while the other begs forgiveness. A mother cries. A follower comforts. A centurion has a change of heart. Women mourn. Leaders smugly taunt. People gawk. Passersby are convicted. Jesus utters the words, "Father, forgive them."

By sundown, the battle was over, but the price was high. The enemy was defeated, and freedom was won for all of those enslaved by sin and its results. A Christian can hardly envision this scene without a sense of conviction, wonder, and gratitude.

Every prayer we utter is a privilege made possible by this sacrifice. Any victory won on behalf of the king and his kingdom began on this eternal battlefield. Hymns and praise songs lifted up throughout churches all over the world every week are the result and celebration of this death. Forgiveness of sin is made possible because of the ultimate price. Jesus had said while he was alive, "Greater love has no one than this, that he lay down his life for his friends" (John 15:13). He lived this out by buying our freedom on the cross.

In the midst of his argument for freedom, Paul is inspired to write two of his most famous verses. In them he shares how freedom's price affects his everyday journey with God and subsequently affects ours. In this chapter, we will reexamine the price Jesus paid for our freedom. Then we will discuss how this calls for us to be crucified with him, live by faith, and hold grace near.

Read Galatians 2:20 & 21 together as a group.

The Cross

Paul begins this teaching by telling his listeners that he has been crucified with Christ. This statement reveals Paul's heart. It conveys a belief that Jesus' death on the cross is the focal point of the freedom gospel. Paul didn't say, "I have been laughed at with Christ." He didn't say, "I have walked on water with Christ." "I have been tempted with Christ," doesn't have the same weight. Paul could have aligned himself with the Messiah in a variety of ways, but he chose the crucifixion. Why? It was the crucifixion of Christ that secured this freedom he was defending. Why would he confront Peter for his exclusion of Gentile Christians as in the last chapter? Because the cross demanded it. What kind of faith does he call for in the chapter that follows? Faith in a savior who would die for those he loved. In these two verses he exposes his deep theology: a Christian's freedom is in the cross, and his life is forever linked to it.

> A Christian's freedom is in the cross, and his life is forever linked to it.

Paul had a lot to say about the crucifixion and the work Christ accomplished on the cross. It is a theme that resurfaces again and again throughout all of his writings. He wrote to the Corinthians, "For the message of the cross is foolishness to those who are perishing, but to us who are being saved it is the power of God" (1 Cor 1:18).

To the church in Ephesus he would write, "In him we have redemption through his blood, the forgiveness of sins, in accordance with the riches of God's grace" (Eph 1:7).

In his Philippian letter he says, "For, as I have often told you and now say again even with tears, many live as enemies of the cross of Christ. Their destiny is destruction, their god is their stomach, and their glory is in their shame" (Phil 3:18-19).

In Colosse these words were read: "For God was pleased to have all his fullness dwell in him, and through him to reconcile to himself all things, whether on earth or things in heaven, by making peace through his blood, shed on the cross" (Col 1:19-20).

To the Christians living in the town of Thessalonica he continues the theme, "They tell how you turned to God from idols to serve the living and true God and to wait for his Son from heaven, whom he raised from the dead—Jesus, who rescues us from the coming wrath" (1 Thess 1:9-10).

These are only a sampling of his teachings on the centrality of the cross to the freedom message. From these Scriptures we can gain a pretty strong picture of what Paul thought of the cross: 1) Paul thought the cross was powerful. He believed the freedom that was accomplished there surpassed any earthly strength. 2) Paul thought the cross was *the* redemptive act. He believed that freedom came because Jesus paid the price there for all sins. 3) Paul understood the cross to have enemies. He believed that those failing to come to the cross were living a life of eternal slavery. 4) Paul thought the cross was the ultimate peace treaty. He saw the work there as reconciling all creation to God—turning slaves into sons. 5) Paul understood the rescuing nature of the cross. He believed that God's wrath would someday bring justice, and only those covered by the blood would survive.

Take a few moments to meditate on these ideas and what they mean for your life, but don't stop there. The cross is not something to be observed, it is something to be embraced, and that's why Paul says he's been crucified with Christ.

> The cross is not something to be observed, it is something to be embraced.

Our Crucifixion

The idea that we would die with Christ was not a new one. From the beginning of his ministry, Jesus himself had said, ". . . anyone who does not carry his cross and follow me cannot be my disciple" (Luke 14:27). No one could have heard those words and not associated Christ-following with death. The cross was a symbol of death, and anyone who carried one was on his way to execution. Jesus taught that his followers would have to lay down their lives to be a part of his kingdom.

But what does it mean to be crucified with Christ? For Paul, of course, it meant the possibility of physical death. Since his message was so countercultural, he lived in the reality that every day could be his last. When he wrote to the Corinthians, "I die every day" (1 Cor 15:31), he meant that he prepared himself for death every day. And he certainly came close many times. In another place he writes, "I bear on my body the marks of our Lord Jesus Christ" (Gal 6:17). History, in fact, gives us clues that he was killed by Caesar's hand in Rome. How then are you and I crucified with Christ?

Although thousands of people lose their lives for faith in Jesus every year worldwide, it is unlikely that most American Christians will actually ever give their lives for what they believe. However, we can be crucified with Christ by embracing the same attitudes that Paul did when it came to dying with Christ.

Christians living in 21st-century America can still die daily. This is simply a determination to live every day as though it will be our last. If today were the last day of our lives, how would our walk with God be different? Who would we tell the freedom story of Jesus to? How would we nurture our spouses and children? How much time would we spend in prayer? What might we write to leave for future generations as a bit of wisdom? Where would we go and what would we say? What would be important and what would be meaningless? Being crucified with Christ is an awareness that today may be the last day and living our lives accordingly.

> Being crucified with Christ is an awareness that today may be the last day and living our lives accordingly.

Christians living in the 21st century can still bear the marks of Jesus. Of course, Paul had scars to show for his beatings, stonings, and mission trip shipwreck. You and I probably will never experience this kind of physical harm because of our faith. However, the scars of our Lord and of the apostles were symbols of sacrifice, and we can do that. We are called to live lives that daily ask, "What can I give up for God?" Can we give away more time, more personal dreams, more service, more money, and more possessions? Are we, in fact, giving up anything for the freedom we have found in Christ? Remember, in Paul's economy, embracing this freedom message meant embracing the cross and the sacrifice that necessarily follows.

> Are we, in fact, giving up anything for the freedom we have found in Christ?

When we begin to live life like it is the day we will die and make daily sacrifices according to those priorities, then we will be able to say with the apostle, "I no longer live, but Christ lives in me." Then life becomes a journey of faith, relying on grace.

Since we will spend the following chapter examining a life of faith, we will only touch on it briefly here. There are two main points to be made about faith and freedom's price. First of all, we need to be reminded that the idea of paying for our sins was God's idea. God didn't wait until judgment day and then watch us squirm uncomfortably as all of our sins were revealed. He didn't allow us to hear the sentence of eternal death handed down in a cold and lonely courtroom. Long before you and I had the chance to hit the floor and beg the Almighty for mercy, God decided he would grant it. The apostle John reminds us,

"This is love: not that we loved God, but that he loved us and sent his son . . ." (1 John 4:10). Faith in the Son of God is a deep heart conviction that God chose to love us.

It is also a belief that Jesus paid the price willingly. Have you ever considered what might have happened if God loved us and even felt pity on us, but was unwilling to pay the price? Many people will cringe at the sight of an animal struck by a car. Some will cry, most will feel pity, but few will stop to see if they can save the creature. Most motorists simply slow down, mutter a "that's sad," and then continue on their journey. What if God saw our plight and drove on by? Thankfully, he didn't. "God so loved the world that He gave his only Son . . ." we read in John 3:16. And Jesus was willing to bear the burden. Paul would later write, ". . . he humbled himself and became obedient to death—even death on a cross" (Phil 2:8). My faith is in a Savior who willingly took the steps to secure my freedom. This is grace.

Paul wants the Galatian Christians to know that we shouldn't set aside grace for some other belief system, philosophy, or religion. We need grace. If we could get right by ourselves or settle our account with God by paying for our sins, Jesus wouldn't have had to die. But he did, because we couldn't get right and we couldn't pay. Grace gives us the freedom that we did not deserve and could not earn. The cross was the eternal payoff, and Paul lived in that awareness every day.

I have had the privilege of traveling to many Spanish-speaking countries throughout my ministry and in that time have learned to communicate on the most basic level. Two years of high school Spanish and several weeks in Mexico, The Dominican Republic, and Puerto Rico have given me a limited vocabulary. In any of these places I can get food, find a bathroom, hail a taxi, give Christian greetings, and understand some of the conversation.

One of the most useful Spanish words I know is the word, "Cuanto?" It is a very simple way of saying, "How much (does it cost)?" This word comes in handy on the inevitable market day included in most short-term mission experiences. Whether you want to buy a painting in Santiago, a hat in Mexico City, or a pound of coffee in San Juan, simply pointing to the object and asking, "Cuanto?" will get you a price. It is an important word. You can't buy anything without knowing the price. Of course, you have to translate pesos into dollars to make sure you know exactly how much you are paying in your currency, but with some simple math you can usually find an object's worth.

Paul reminds us here that the freedom that you and I long for deep within came at a price. When we think of living free from the consequences of all the wrong things we have ever done; when we dream of a life free from all the loneliness, emptiness, and pain this world has to offer; and when we long for an eternal home where we will be free to love and be loved, we are reminded that there is a price. How much? The answer lies in the cross of Christ! 3:16

3 *Freedom's Price*

Living Free

1. If you were to assign a monetary amount to represent the sin of your life, what would be the price of your sin? Why?

2. If you saw yourself as facing crucifixion every day, how would that affect your life? How would you treat those around you? Where would you go? What would you talk about?

3. Spend some time thanking God for sending the perfect sacrifice for your sin. Remember the price he paid by celebrating communion together as a group.

4. What have you given up for Jesus lately?

5. Decide to sacrifice something over the next 30 days in order to grow closer to God. For example: give up your favorite TV show for a month and replace that with Bible reading or prayer.

| **Memory Verse** Gal 2:20 | *I have been crucified with Christ and I no longer live, but Christ lives in me. The life I live in the body, I live by faith in the Son of God, who loved me and gave himself for me.* |

CHAPTER FOUR

FREEDOM THROUGH FAITH

GALATIANS 3:1-14

It is difficult to accept a free gift. That may sound absurd to you, but if you'll observe people in social settings, you'll find it to be true. People don't really like getting free things. It seems to be human nature to reject something that wasn't earned or is undeserved. There are four common statements that reflect this attitude. I've heard them and said them hundreds of times; maybe you'll recognize them.

1. "You shouldn't have."

This is the statement someone makes when they receive an unexpected gift. You might see this at a baby shower, when, instead of the obligatory bottles, a year's supply of diapers, and clothes with feet in them, the mother-to-be receives an expensive car seat/carrier. It wasn't on the list and

> It seems to be human nature to reject something that wasn't earned or is undeserved.

was totally unexpected, and so the recipient politely says, "Oh, you shouldn't have." A very close relative of this statement is, "You didn't have to do that." These statements reveal a feeling of unworthiness on the part of the one receiving the gift. They may love the gift and inwardly be excited to have it, but they will still act as if they are not worthy of the gift.

2. "But I didn't get you anything."

You might hear this when an anniversary rolls around. The wife has secretly planned a nice dinner and a movie and has purchased her husband a new shirt and a favorite CD. After dinner, she presents her carefully wrapped gifts with a card. The husband was surprised by the dinner, but the gifts remind him that he forgot to give her a gift. He stammers, ". . . but, I didn't get you anything." This is his way of saying, "I can't repay you." This gift is difficult to accept because now the husband feels as if he owes something he can't make up for. He can't go back and buy her a gift; it will be too late. Many times this is preceded by phrase number one creating the combination idea of unworthiness and inability to repay.

3. "Let me get that, you bought last time."

I live in a town where eating out is commonplace. Consequently, many of the ministry meetings, prayer groups, and planning sessions that I'm involved in take place in restaurants all over the city. Most of these meals include laughter, good food, coffee, discussion, encouragement, and of course, the bill. The fun begins when the waitress lays the bill face down on the table. Often two or three people make an effort to buy for the others, and that's when you'll most likely hear, "Let me get that, you bought last time." Now, on the surface, it sounds noble. One guy shouldn't buy all the time, so this phrase lets the other know that he is willing to pick up the tab sometimes. But what he's really saying is, "I'm keeping score." The implication is "I never want you to get ahead of me in meal-buying so I'm keeping track."

4. "You spent way too much on me."

This sometimes happens when good friends decide to exchange gifts for Christmas. For some reason one sees a gift that costs a little more than what she might normally spend, but it is "just so her." At the time of the exchange, the unsuspecting recipient opens her expensive gift. She knows it's expensive and she knows hers isn't in the same price range, so she instinctively blurts out, "You spent way too much on me." This is in the same "unworthiness" family as the first statement, but more definitive. This statement from one who has been given a gift reflects that he or she feels unworthy, and he or she knows the price. People may think they deserved something (after all, it is an exchange), but not something worth that much.

These statements are not relegated to everyday situations like those above. I believe that these statements reveal our spiritual emotions as well. This is the trouble with grace. God gives us this incredible gift through Jesus, and we respond by telling him he shouldn't have because we are unworthy. I have had all too many people sit in my office and wonder out loud whether or not God could forgive "even them." Not only do most of us struggle with our unworthiness, but we are keenly aware of the score, and we know we can't repay this kindness. Many people come to Christ desiring to earn what he has freely given. They spend a lifetime of beating themselves up because they can never even the score with God. Grace is free and there is only way to respond to it—believe.

Read Galatians 3:1-14 together as a group.
Pray and ask God to teach you about faith.

Along with Moses and Isaiah, you couldn't get a bigger Old Testament star than Abraham. Of course, he was the one who received the original covenant with God that he would become the father of many nations and all people on the earth would be blessed through him (see verse 8 in the passage you just read). As Paul continues his discussion on this incredible gift of freedom, he uses Abraham as an example of one who accepted this gift by faith and not by works. As we examine his story, we will learn about our own story.

God appeared to Abraham in a town called Ur and told him that he was chosen. At that moment God gave him the greatest gift ever imagined. From that point on, the Almighty promised to be his God. In chapter 12 of Genesis he covenanted with Abraham:

"I will make you into a great nation and I will bless you;
I will make your name great, and you will be a blessing.
I will bless those who bless you, and whoever curses you I will curse;
And all peoples on earth will be blessed through you" (Gen 12:1-3).

God gave Abraham an incredible gift. God would give him more children than the stars in the sky or the sands on the beach. God would make him famous. God would help him prosper. God would destroy his enemies. God would bless the world through him. God would be his God. If it sounds too good to be true, this is the way God deals with people.

Abraham was given all of these things for free. Was Abraham completely unworthy? Yes. Would he ever be able to work off the debt of gratitude that this gift demanded? No way. What was the score here in the game of giving gifts? God–a million, Abraham–zero. So what did Abraham do in response to this gift?

What he didn't do was try to earn it or "try to attain (his) goal by human effort" (read verse five again). Abraham didn't begin to follow a bunch of rules when God made this promise. He didn't begin a ritualistic religion based on special words, times, and celebrations. He didn't change the way he lived. He kept on being Abraham.

What took place in Abraham on the day God spoke with him was totally internal and spiritual. He believed that the words God had spoken would come true. If you want to know what Abraham did physically, we can only guess. He probably packed everything he owned onto the back of some donkeys and camels for the long journey ahead. He may have looked at Sarah romantically and wondered when she would be pregnant with the promised child. More than likely, he took long walks at night and stared at the stars a lot.

Abraham was not righteous because of some immediate life change. Abraham had faith and that's what made him righteous. He wasn't immediately circumcised; that would come later. No one referred to him as Hebrew, Jewish, or Israelite. He had no yearly feasts or fasts to comply with. He believed, plain and simple, and when it comes to freedom in Christ, there is nothing we can do to earn it, repay it, or even the score. We are simply called to believe.

For the rest of this chapter we are going to look at how this life of faith is lived out. Paul is saying the path to freedom is in Abraham's footsteps, and it's by faith, not by observing the law, as some of his detractors were claiming. In these verses, he reveals two parts to living out faith. The person of faith lives by the Spirit not the flesh, and that faith is credited not earned.

Freedom through Faith Is Lived by the Spirit, Not the Flesh.

The apostle teaches the Galatians that freedom by faith is first and foremost a work of the Holy Spirit. He reminds them that they received the Spirit by believing and not by doing something. He recalls that they began with the Spirit on this walk to freedom. And he reiterates that the Spirit is the source of the miracles they have witnessed (see Gal 3:2-5). When the Galatians from Antioch had heard the freedom gospel for the first time, they responded by wanting more and encouraging the apostles to continue preaching their message. They invited nearly everyone in the city to come and hear the good news (see Acts 13:42-44). This was not a work of the law, it was the power of the Holy Spirit to convict and move in people's hearts.

When the Galatians from Lystra saw the man who was lame from birth walking around, the entire town was riveted to the messengers of freedom (see Acts 14:3,8-10). Paul is reminding them in this teaching that healings were a result of the Holy Spirit and had nothing to do with obedience to Moses' teachings. If their conversion was anything like other New Testament believers', their baptisms into Christ were accompanied by the Spirit's indwelling.

Paul is giving them a very personal spiritual history. The churches of Galatia began this journey to freedom by the Holy Spirit's power, healing, and indwelling. Why, the apostle wondered, would they now go to something else? Paul is encouraging them that faith is a spiritual thing, not an outward-action thing. The miracles they first experienced weren't the result of being religious or being circumcised or any other outward show of piety. The Spirit moved them toward righteousness.

This was the same beginning that the "father of faith," Abraham, experienced. We aren't told how this first meeting with God actually happened. Genesis twelve simply says that, "the Lord had said to Abram . . ." (Gen 12:1). What we do know is that the Holy Spirit must have been a part of this calling. It is not a stretch, as evidenced in other Bible movements of God, to assume that the Holy Spirit was there stirring the heart of Abraham. Paul's point is that Abraham didn't begin by being a follower of God's rules or through any other human effort. Moses was still generations away, and even though Terah and his sons may have been worshipers of the God of their ancestry, it was this conversation with God that began Abraham's faith walk. It was a Spirit move that revealed God. And when the Spirit moved, Abraham believed. This is the same way the Galatians began, with the Spirit. It is the same for us.

We began with the Holy Spirit. It is the Holy Spirit that is the identifying mark of every Christian. The writer of Romans says, "If anyone does not have the Spirit of Christ, he does not belong to him" (see Rom 8:9). It is the Holy Spirit that moves in us to help us conform to Christ's likeness. The Holy Spirit guides us. The Holy Spirit comforts us and pleads our case when we can only groan. To accept the Holy Spirit is to reject the notion that we can attain freedom on our own. The life of faith is contingent on "keeping in step with the Spirit" (Gal 5:25).

> To accept the Holy Spirit is to reject the notion that we can attain freedom on our own.

This means we are called to have faith that the Holy Spirit is able to do all of those things we talked about earlier. We don't like free gifts when we feel unworthy, but it is the Spirit whose very indwelling makes us worthy. We don't like free gifts when we know we can't pay them back, but the Spirit guarantees that we don't need to pay God back. The Spirit living in our lives is a testimony that God isn't keeping score.

> God isn't keeping score.

So many Christians struggle with the gift of God's grace. Many set up spiritual programs to try harder, to pray more, and to be more religious.

Of course, these are good intentions, but they set us up for failure. True Christian living is going through every day with an attentive ear to the Holy Spirit, allowing him to grow, mature, and develop godly character in us. Perhaps a picture from marriage will help us grasp this idea.

Men, by nature, are slobs. This may not be true for all, but a quick trip through any guys' college dormitory would most often reinforce this generalization. In a man's world, it is normal to leave dirty dishes around for days. It is normal to throw clothes on the floor, only to pick them up a week later for reuse. A man will not think twice about drinking directly from the milk carton or wearing clothes that don't match. Making the bed for most men is a waste of time. It's not that every man's mom hasn't told him the rules or tried to change his behavior. It's just that the default mode for most guys is the slob mode.

What changes a man is marriage. Watch men who have been married for a long time, and you will find guys who are picking up clothes, washing dishes, clearing the table, drinking from a glass, and putting the lid down. What happened? Years of living with a creature called woman has rubbed off. Hopefully, on their wedding day, she didn't present him with a list of do's and don'ts. In all likelihood, the wife hasn't demanded that he perform certain duties every day in order to receive love and affection. But the man has undeniably changed as the marriage has matured. How did this happen? The change wasn't an outward change, it was inward. The marriage relationship has brought about change over time based on a relationship of love.

In the same way, by nature we are sinners. We will lie, cheat, steal, gossip, and curse. We will be impatient, selfish, and materialistic every time we get the chance. Sinning is the human default mode. Faith does not come by following a list of rules that God has established. History has proven that sooner or later humans will break the rules. This is what Paul teaches in this portion of the letter: trying to obtain righteousness by following the rules only condemns us. He writes, "Cursed is everyone who does not continue to do everything written in the Book of the Law" (Gal 3:10). If you can't keep all of the law, then you are wasting your time, for failure to keep one law is imperfection and condemnation.

The faith that leads to freedom is living in the presence of the Holy Spirit so that he can change us from within over time. God's presence assures us that this will happen. Righteousness comes by faith not by works. This leads us to the second part of living out our faith.

Freedom through Faith Is Credited, Not Earned.

Most of us have a credit line of some sort. We buy houses, cars, appliances, vacations, furniture, etc. with credit. Many of us use credit cards to fund other purchases like meals, clothes, entertainment, and bill paying. Credit is a simple concept. Some bank or lending institution allows you to be worth more (in purchasing power) than you are really worth. Many of us have gotten credit card offers via the mail. In most of these letters, someone we don't know reveals that we are part of a special offer (along with everyone else in our neighborhood). They are offering a credit card with a low introductory interest rate and with a credit line up to twenty, thirty, or forty thousand dollars. I've actually gotten some of these letters. What these institutions are telling me is that they will allow me to spend $30,000 when I know very well that I'm not worth that much. So goes credit.

On the other hand, I have a job. I am one of the blessed who has the privilege of working for a church. The leaders of my church sign a contract with me every year to pay me a set amount in return for my preaching, leading, serving, pastoring, and helping. On the 15th and 30th day of every month, I expect to receive a paycheck. I have earned it. I am paid what the church has determined I'm worth, and since I signed the contract, I guess I agree.

God's credit is the same. Another look at Abraham and we will see a man who is called righteous. We have to believe that he was because God said he was. But notice how he attained it. He didn't earn his righteousness. It was credited to him (see Gal 3:6). In effect, God was saying to Abraham, you'll never earn a righteousness paycheck by your actions, but if you believe in me I'll give you a credit line for righteousness.

Paul communicates to his readers that this is the way they can be righteous. He says in verse nine of our reading that those who have faith are blessed along with Abraham. The opposition teachers were proposing that circumcision and following the law tied us to Abraham's righteousness. Paul's freedom message, however, stated that we are linked with Abraham by our faith. We must believe that we are righteous by the Spirit of God living in us and by the credit that God has given us. ⌷3:16⌷

Living Free

1. What is the best gift you ever received? (You may have more than one.) Who gave you this gift and why was it so significant? How did you feel when you received this gift?

2. What changes has the Holy Spirit brought into your life over time because of your love relationship with God?

3. Which response best describes your reaction to God's free gift? "You shouldn't have." "But I didn't get you anything." "Let me get that, you bought last time." Or "you spent way too much on me." Why?

4. How do you sometimes try to live out your faith walk in the flesh? (I.e., what do you do to try to earn God's love?)

Memory Verse
Gal 3:6

Consider Abraham: "He believed God, and it was credited to him as righteousness."

CHAPTER FIVE

FREEDOM AND THE LAW

GALATIANS 3:19-25

Sometimes the law doesn't seem to make sense. If you've ever spent five minutes waiting for a light to turn green at 1:00 a.m. when there is not another car for miles, you'll probably agree. If you've ever noticed the label on a mattress that warns against removing said label, you've probably questioned why that law exists. If you've ever wondered why there is Braille on a drive-through ATM, some law has required it to be so. Sometimes we encounter laws and wonder why they were written.

If you conduct a quick search on the internet, you can discover all kinds of laws. One can only guess as to why some of the following were written:

In Alaska it is illegal to push a moose out of a flying plane.

This begs the question, "What was a moose doing in an airplane?" Did a moose land in someone's backyard, endangering children at play? Maybe the skydiving moose came through the roof of some legislator's home and scared his wife. The next time, the lawmakers in Alaska got together, there it was: the "No-flying-moose" law. That's not the only strange airplane law. Check out the next one.

In Lowes Crossroads, Delaware, it is illegal for a pilot or a passenger to carry an ice cream cone in his pocket while either flying or waiting to board a plane.

Again, was this law precipitated by some crazy ice-cream event? Did someone, after being told that he would not be able to take his cone on board, try to smuggle it on board in his pocket? Can you imagine?

Then, he gets to his seat only to notice a telltale drip of ice cream from the pilot's pocket. The injustice of it all causes him to call his legislator immediately after landing.

Trenton, New Jersey, has a law that says it's illegal to throw tainted pickles into the street.

Is this law in response to a car wreck caused when someone swerved to miss a pile of pickles? Or was it written in earlier times when either a horse or a beggar became seriously ill after digesting the discarded dills? It certainly would be an interesting arrest: "Sir, I'm going to have to take you downtown for illegal distribution of pickles in an unauthorized zone." Imagine the shame of being labeled a relish tray offender!

The state of Oregon has a law prohibiting the use of canned corn for fishing.

Picture a couple of your stereotypical fishermen. They come complete with old hats, fishing vests with hooks in them, and an old boat. It's a beautiful Oregon day on the lake and the fish are biting. Never mind that for some reason, these two brought a can of corn along for the trip. At some point, one of them decided to either use it as bait or throw it at fish as they swam close to the boat. At any rate, I think we'll all agree that the world is a better place without this sort of nonsense.

What Was *That* About?

There are many laws in our society that cause one to wonder why, but the Bible also has its share of puzzling rules. A casual read through the Old Testament laws may seem just as humorous as the ones listed above. We're not talking about the Ten Commandments here; laws condemning murder, lying, adultery, and coveting all make perfectly good sense. But if you look at some of the more obscure laws written in Leviticus and Deuteronomy, you may wonder what God was thinking:

Do not wear clothing woven of two kinds of material (Lev 19:19).

Is this some kind of law designed to keep our fathers from going out in public with clothes that don't match? Does God have an eye for fashion?

Do not cut the hair at the sides of your head or clip off the edges of your beard. (Lev 19:27).

Was God this concerned with the facial hair of Israelite men? Is God like so many fathers who want their sons to wear a certain kind of haircut? Was Elvis onto something?

Make tassels on the four corners of the cloak you wear (Deut 21:12).

Yet another fashion rule given to us by the Almighty? Maybe this was a special gown designed to match the graduation cap tassels. It

47

‡

C
H
A
P
T
E
R

Freedom and the Law 5

does seem a bit strange that a bunch of tent dwellers would wear clothes with such fancy additions.

If you enter your neighbor's vineyard, you may eat all the grapes you want, but do not put any in your basket (Deut 23:24).

This is a great law for fans of jelly and grape juice. No matter how poor you were, you could always find a meal on the vine. And like most all-you-can-eat places, doggie bags were forbidden.

As you can see, the law was made up of much more than the commandments Moses received in the mountain, rules concerning circumcision, and the dates for yearly feasts. When one considers that "the law" to the first-century Jew included the entirety of the Old Testament, the Mishnah (oral traditions and judgments of respected rabbis), and the Midrash (rabbinic interpretations of the O.T. Scriptures); the complexity of rules is overwhelming.

To understand the absurd proportions to which Jewish leaders had taken their traditions, one need look no further than a confrontation Jesus had with a group of Pharisees in Matthew 23:23. Jesus takes note that these religious leaders followed the tithing regulations for literally everything they owned: "You give a tenth of your spices—mint, dill, and cumin." Can you imagine going through your kitchen cabinets to give a tenth of your spices? This is only one example of how the law had become overwhelming in its scope. Even in this instance, Jesus notes that these religious guys are missing the heart behind the law.

This is why Paul dedicated much of the first part of his letter to the Galatian churches arguing that they were not bound to keep the Law. As we have discussed, he contended that they were free from the Law (in its extensive, expanded form) along with its accompanying customs, rituals, and festivals. Paul's freedom gospel was to the Gentiles and he was certain their place in the kingdom was not contingent on their adherence to rules.

This leads us to an interesting question. Why was the Law written? Obviously, God was the author of these laws. Could it be that they were bad laws? Were these laws ineffective? Or had they become outdated? Today many Christians wonder what the Old Testament has to do with our lives in Christ. On one hand we are not called to follow the law, and on the other it makes up two-thirds of our Bible. Do we need Genesis through Malachi? And if we do need it, what are we to do with it?

Paul asks these two very important questions with slightly different wording in this segment of his letter: "What, then, was the purpose of the law?" (Gal 3:19) and "Is the law, therefore, opposed to the promises of God?" (Gal 3:21). This sets up his discussion for freedom's correlation with the law. Over the next couple of pages we will learn from the apostle what purpose the law held and how it in no way contradicts the promises of God.

Read Galatians 3:15-25 in preparation for our study.

Before addressing the meaning and usefulness of the law, Paul wants his readers to recall where the law fell historically. He reminds them in the verses we just read that God made a covenant with Abraham long before any law was ever given. As a matter of fact, it was 430 years after God told Abraham he would be the father of many nations that God told Moses to come up in the mountain. The covenant and the promise that went with it could not be eclipsed by laws which followed. He uses first-century judiciary language to illustrate his point. In Paul's day, a legal covenant between two people would not permit alterations or additions. Once the agreement was made, the conditions of the contract were legally binding. In the same way, God's covenant with Abraham could not be altered by the law. Once God established the covenant, it was destined to happen. God's promise would be kept.

Remember, the main promise was to Abraham and to his seed. The word "seed" was a prophecy of a future relative—understood by the apostles to be Jesus. God made Abraham a promise of family, of prosperity, and that these blessings would in turn bless all people. This promise culminated in the life of Jesus Christ. This is what God had in mind long before he gave his people laws to follow in the wilderness and beyond. When God made all of these promises to Abraham, he had a plan to send his son Jesus to save the world. The covenant and the promise supersede the law. Which brings us back to our original question: Why the law? There are three reasons the law is an integral part of our freedom.

The Law Was Given as a Guide to Life

Just because laws don't seem to make sense doesn't mean that they are wrong. Most of our parents had a rule that prohibited playing in the street. Many of us were told several times not to play with matches. Nearly every parent warned against talking to strangers. These were rules or laws given to us at an early age. Many of us wondered why or doubted the reasoning behind these parental demands. We may not have even liked the rules, but now that we are older, we see their validity.

In the same way, many of God's laws may not seem to make sense until you look a little closer. God's laws were established for our good. In his book *Right from Wrong* Josh McDowell comments on this quality of God's Word, "Like a two-edged sword, God's words—His commands and judgments—cut both ways. They accomplish our good by a 'two-edged' process: they protect and provide. In the words of the Lord to Jeremiah, His commands are intended to 'prosper' us (provide) and 'not to harm' us (protect)."[1]

When God gave regulations about mildew, he was protecting the camp from disease. When he made laws about unclean foods, he was prohibiting foods that were high in fat or may spoil. When he said to circumcise your sons on the eighth day, he knew that is when an infant's body becomes efficient at blood clotting. Even the regulations about wearing clothes made of wool and linen sewn together are practical. God knew such clothing wouldn't be conducive to a nomadic lifestyle. When he commanded homeowners to build a wall around the roof of their houses, he was preventing people from falling. God made laws to meet the needs of his people while keeping them from harm.

Our reading today goes further with this idea of the law guiding us. Paul mentions in our reading that the law "was added because of transgressions." The law was given as a guide to life because the lives of humans were filled with sin. The tendency of humans to do wrong, called for some sort of discipline until God delivered us through the promised Seed. The laws were a direct result of the sinfulness of the people. The commandments were God's way of setting a standard by which we could measure right and wrong. Without the law, humankind would spiral out of control into a world of lawlessness, chaos, and fear. Any historical examination of a nation or people living outside the context of established laws will reveal complete destruction. God knew that sin would utterly destroy his people if he didn't give them rules to live by.

> God knew that sin would utterly destroy his people if he didn't give them rules to live by.

The Law Was Given to Strengthen the Promise

Remember that the promise (God's promise to Abraham) was more important than the covenant itself. However, God gave the law to strengthen the promise. When the Seed arrived on earth, he said, "Do not think that I have come to abolish the Law or the Prophets; I have not come to abolish them, but to fulfill them" (Matt 5:17). So how did Jesus strengthen and fulfill the law, and how did the law in turn strengthen the promise?

First of all, the law strengthens the promise because it plainly showed people the concept of sin. Rules and commands are standards of right, and when people break those rules, it proves they are wrong. When people break these rules over and over again, it proves that they are incapable of doing right. It proves that the power of sin is more powerful than those who are called to follow the law. This is why Paul says in Galatians 3:22 that "the Scripture declares that the whole world is a prisoner to sin."

Have you ever heard someone talk about his inability to overcome a habit? Many Christians struggle with overeating, smoking, or controlling the words they say. Why is it that a person who desires to control his appetite eats a half gallon of Breyer's mint chocolate chip ice cream? (Does this sound like a confession?) Why would someone who knows it is harmful to smoke struggle with quitting? Why would someone who wants to glorify God with all of her life, let out of a string of expletives in a tense moment? The answer lies in our propensity to sin.

As much as we try to do right, we often do the wrong instead. The apostle could relate to our plight. Paul writes in another place, "I do not understand what I do. For what I want to do I do not do, but what I hate I do" (Rom 7:15). He goes on to explain that this is a result of sin living in him. So, the law serves its purpose in that it plainly reveals to us that we are sinners in need of a Savior. The law clearly shows us our slavery to sin, which means that it proves that we can never live freely while we are bound to follow the law. We need the promise of God to free us.

The law also strengthened the promise because it pointed to the eternal. The law itself was not made to last. It was established for temporary living. It was designed for the desert but it illustrated life in the Promised Land. The circumcision mark in Hebrew males pointed to a people set apart for God. The cleanliness rules of the desert pointed to a holy nation. The yearly feasts were designed to represent and foreshadow the plentiful provision of God. The people lived in the desert, but they longed for a better place. God designed laws for his people that would point them to a time and place where he lived among them.

Even the way we received the law speaks to its temporary nature. In the Old Testament Moses reminded the people, "At that time I stood between the Lord and you to declare to you the word of the Lord" (Deut 5:5). He is the mediator that Paul refers to in Galatians 3:19. The law was put into effect by a man representing both people to God and God to people. Moses was God's spokesman for rules, but God speaks for himself when it comes to the covenant. That's what Paul means when he says God is one. When it comes to the promise and eternal things, God speaks through his son Jesus, who was the promised seed. The temporary law, given by a temporary man, pointed to an eternal promise fulfilled in the Eternal Man, Christ Jesus.

Finally, the law strengthened the promise because it provided the context for the salvation story. We sometimes forget that human history is a story. The story began when God breathed man into existence, and it culminates when he comes to take his people to live with him eternally. In between, we have stories of God and man. These stories, from Adam and Eve to yours and mine, are the context for God's salvation.

The law was given to those who lived under the Old Covenant to illustrate the priesthood—the role of representation for people before God. The law was established by the mouths of prophets speaking the word of God. The law was the rule for great kings who led God's people throughout the Old Testament. If we didn't have an understanding of priests, prophets, and kings in the context of the law, then we wouldn't understand Jesus' role as Prophet, Priest, and King. It is within the context of God's story "at just the right time" when we are introduced to the main character—our Lord Jesus. This leads us to our last purpose.

The Law Was Given to Point Us to Jesus

The Old Testament laws point us to freedom through Jesus. The idea of a blood sacrifice to take away sins began with bulls and goats but culminated in Christ on a cross. The ceremonial purity required by a priest entering God's presence was fulfilled in the sinless, pure life of his Son. The rules protecting the innocent and helpless were a physical illustration of how Jesus would rescue those who were helpless because of their sin. Crying out for a deliverer because of the oppression and slavery in a foreign land is a precursor to a cry for the Messiah to relieve the oppressed. Nearly every law in the Old Testament reflects the glory and perfection of God which in turn is embodied in the person of Christ.

According to Paul, the law not only pointed us to Jesus, it was put in charge to make sure we got to Jesus. The Greek word used in Galatians 3:24 is "pedagogue." This word described a slave whose job it was to oversee a child's inheritance until that child was of age. This person was to watch over the affairs and estate of the master's child until he reached maturity. Once the child reached a specific age, the pedagogue had no more authority over him.

The picture is that of the law watching over mankind until Jesus came. Until faith in Christ came, we needed the law to guide us in the things of God, but since Jesus opened up relationship with God through faith, we no longer need to be supervised by the law. We are mature enough to receive God by faith.

When Paul preached freedom from the law, he was not advocating doing away with the law. He believed and taught that God's law had a purpose in bringing us to Christ. He didn't believe that the law was in opposition to the promise but that it in fact supported the promised Seed. This means that we as Christians must be interested in the Old Testament Scriptures because they are a part of the story of Jesus. The law is not freedom, but it is a part of the journey there. 3:16

> The law is not freedom, but it is a part of the journey there.

---

[1] Josh McDowell, *Right from Wrong* (Dallas: Word, 1994) 109.

Living Free

1. Spend some time listing rules that you have specific to your house, your church, your workplace, or your school. What would any of these places be without rules?

2. Take time this week to write your God story. Be sure to include the journey before and after Christ touched your life. Who in the Old Testament or New Testament does your story most resemble?

3. Read through the laws in Exodus, Leviticus, and Deuteronomy. Try to find as many correlations between Jesus and these laws as you can.

| **Memory Verse** Gal 3:24-25 | *So the law was put in charge to lead us to Christ that we might be justified by faith. [25] Now that faith has come, we are no longer under the supervision of the law.* |

CHAPTER SIX

FREEDOM BY RELATIONSHIP

GALATIANS 3:26-29 / 4:21-31

Family membership has its privileges. I grew up the son of a preacher, who was the son of a farmer. My grandfather was an honest man who worked hard and lived simply. He had thick fingers attached to powerful hands. Overalls and a farmer's cap were his style and early-to-late was his work ethic. In the summertime, my siblings and I usually spent a week or two with Grandma and Grandpa on their Indiana farm. This was a special treat, especially for city kids.

In those times we rode the tractor (when I was older, I got to drive it!), pulled weeds in the garden, took naps in the shade of the huge oak trees, and snapped a lot of green beans. At mealtimes we got to sit and listen to wisdom that only a wizened farmer can offer. Grandma cooked and baked all day, and we usually helped her. On the weekends we went with them to church and endured the comments and pinches associated with "getting so big." These are only a few memories that mean so much to me as I reflect on my life. I consider the influence my grandparents had on my life to be my true inheritance: a legacy of faith and family. And with their simple ways and humble means, that's all I ever expected. Little did I know that I would inherit something more.

Later, over a period of fourteen years, my grandma passed away, followed by my father, an estranged uncle, and finally my grandpa. Each death brought the sting the Scripture speaks of, but we got through like most people do with support from family, friends, and faith in God. With each passing, it was common (if not a bit irreverent) to find ourselves sitting in some church fellowship hall joking about some fictitious inheritance. I say joke, because we all knew that none of our relatives were wealthy enough to leave something behind. That's why it came as such a shock when I received a letter informing me that I would be receiving a check from Grandpa's estate. Actually, all I cared about were some photos, an old pocket watch of Grandpa's, and some drinking glasses Grandma had. Apparently, I was also entitled to some money.

We finally figured out that the estranged uncle (I hadn't seen him in seven years before his death) had accumulated some wealth in his lifetime. At the time of his unexpected death, he had no wife and no will, so his estate went to my grandfather. Grandpa was already in a nursing home at this point, and I'm not sure if he really understood what it all meant. When Grandpa passed away, the inheritance money from my uncle that had been passed on to his father now came to the next nearest relative—me.

I was an heir, but not because I was Grandpa's favorite. I was not an heir because someone had planned it. I would receive a check from my grandfather's estate simply because a probate judge determined that I was the next of kin. I received an inheritance because I was related to the deceased. The name "Baker" associated me with the man who left behind some assets. Family membership has its privileges.

The Family Inheritance

According to Paul, membership in the spiritual family has its privileges as well. As a matter of fact, he points out in this segment of our study that the Christian attains freedom through relationship. We don't earn freedom because of what we do; we inherit freedom because of who we are related to. It is in association with Abraham and his descendants (namely Jesus) that you and I become sons of God and heirs of his kingdom.

> Membership in the spiritual family has its privileges as well.

Read Galatians 3:26-29 and 4:21-31 in preparation for our study.

To fully understand the point the apostle is trying to make, we must understand the history of father Abraham and the sons he had. We used to sing a song in children's church that began, "Father Abraham had many sons" and included, "I am one of them." To help us find our place in the family, we will examine Abraham's family and the role of each of his sons.

In Genesis 16 Abraham is a full ten years into the land of Canaan. It had been a decade of wandering, tents, herds, altars, and reminders of God's ever-present covenant that someday he would be the father of many nations. There was only one problem. Abraham was, according to most scholars, nearing his 86th birthday, and Sarah was just as barren now as when God had called him from Ur. Perhaps Sarah was growing impatient and frustrated, but it was at this point that Sarah took matters into her own hands and decided to help Abraham have his son through purely human methods. Since she was barren, she reasoned, the only viable option was for her to bear children through her Egyptian handmaid Hagar.

Before you pass judgment on Sarah, remember that she was a barren woman. In a culture in which women found their place by bearing children for their husbands to carry on the family name, this was the worst condition a woman could find herself in. Couple this with the fact that for nearly ten years Abraham had been telling anyone and everyone that God had promised to make him the father of many nations, and you may understand her impatience. You may also recall that Abraham himself had suggested another option for inheritance, namely a guy from Damascus named Eliezer (see Gen 15:2-3).

At any rate, Abraham complied with Sarah's wishes, and in no time Hagar was with child. This caused friction and jealousy within Abraham's home, but nine months later a son was born and he named him Ishmael.

Fast-forward another thirteen years. Abraham is now 99 years old and his only son is still Ishmael. Remember again, that Abraham has now been 23 years in the land God told him to go to, and still Sarah is barren. At this point God instituted the covenant mark of circumcision with Abraham and all the males in his household. As God institutes this mark, he reiterates his covenant and again promises Abraham that Sarah will have a son. Abraham can't believe it and has the following conversation with God:

> "Will a son be born to a man a hundred years old? Will Sarah bear a
> child at the age of ninety?" And Abraham said to God, "If only Ishmael
> might live under your blessing!" Then God said, "Yes, but your wife
> Sarah will bear you a son, and you will call him Isaac. I will establish
> my covenant with him as an everlasting covenant for his descendants
> after him" (Gen 17:18-19).

A year later Isaac is born of Sarah, and at age 100 Abraham receives the son that God had promised him all along. This was the son of promise. The covenant was through Isaac. When it was all said and done, Abraham had six sons besides Isaac. Of course, there was Ishmael, but then there were five other sons which Abraham had by Keturah (see Gen 25:1-4). These sons were sons born in the natural way, unlike

Isaac who was born in the extraordinary, supernatural way. And because Isaac was the special son, he received all of the inheritance. "Abraham left everything he owned to Isaac. But while he was still living, he gave gifts to the sons of his concubines and sent them away from his son Isaac to the land of the east" (Gen 25:5-6). Over thirteen hundred years later, Paul uses this family tree to illustrate how Christians are made free by relationship with Abraham.

To the apostle, Hagar figuratively represents the covenant from Mt. Sinai. The law that Moses received there was physically written on stone tablets for the people to follow. Hagar did bear Abraham his first son but this was a purely physical act. When a man and a woman are sexually intimate, procreation is a natural result. The birth of Ishmael was no more miraculous than millions of births in the history of mankind. Like the law, this son was physical, tangible, and very explainable.

Besides this, Hagar was a slave woman, and in eastern cultures the son of a slave was destined to slavery. Of course, Abraham loved his son Ishmael, and may have even loved Hagar, but there was nothing he could do to change the social status of either. They were slaves, and when it came to inheritance and family, a slave had no rights. So Abraham didn't leave anything for Ishmael. Ishmael was not a part of God's spiritual work and therefore was not a part of the spiritual inheritance. He was left out of the will.

Not only was he left out of the will, but he was also prohibited from being in the family physically. At some point, Abraham actually cut off all of his other sons from his presence and away from Isaac. This solidified Isaac's place as the important son for God's plan. Now these actions toward the six sons born in the natural way may seem cold to us today, but these sons simply weren't a part of God's plan. It was God's design to fulfill his promise through Isaac. According to Paul, these natural-born sons are a picture of the Old Covenant. This means we can learn some lessons from their lives.

The Son of the Promise

First of all, the law is like the slave woman Hagar, and therefore anyone born of the law is destined to live a life of slavery. There is no way that freedom can be achieved via the law. No matter how hard Ishmael tried to please his father and become the son of promise, he was just a naturally born slave. In the same way, no matter how hard someone tries to please God by following the law, they will always be enslaved

> No matter how hard someone tries, they will always be enslaved.

by their inability to achieve righteousness. If the law is compared to a slave, the people who follow it will only be seen as children of slavery.

The second thing we learn from Abraham's family tree is that only sons born of the promise of God will receive an inheritance. Can you imagine how it must have been at the reading of Abraham's will? Abraham was a wealthy man, rich in herds, tents, goods, and servants. At one time he had over 318 men who were his property, born of his servants (see Gen 14:14). He could have divided his estate seven ways and made each of his sons very rich. Surely Ishmael would get some property and a few herds; after all he was the oldest (traditionally, this would have entitled him to a double portion of the inheritance). One might think that even Keturah's sons were entitled to a goat or two. But when Abraham died, there was nothing left for these six brothers. All of the land God promised to give Abraham and all that he had accumulated went solely to his son Isaac.

Finally, there was separation between the sons of concubines and the son of the wife through whom God would establish his covenant. As we mentioned earlier, Abraham physically removed his sons to another country. This was at the request of Sarah, upon learning that Ishmael was making fun of Isaac. Paul quotes her from Genesis 21:10: "Get rid of the slave woman and her son, for the slave woman's son will never share in the inheritance with the free woman's son" (Gal 4:30). This was of course more than the overreaction of a protective mother; it was God's plan. All natural offspring had to be separated from the supernatural offspring so that no one would mistake where the Seed to come actually came from. Spiritually, this separates those who are born of the law and those who are born of the promise. The two are not related and therefore have nothing in common. It was the Judaizers who were attempting to exclude Gentile believers from God's family but ironically were themselves excluded.

To summarize the apostle's illustration: We understand God to be the Father of promise. Abraham is the type of God here. Like Abraham, he has an inheritance for those who belong to his spiritual family. We understand that Hagar was the picture of the natural union that begat the law and was born on the mountains of Sinai as the Israelites came out of Egypt. The descendants of this union were those who in the first century resided in the city of Jerusalem and protected the identity of their slave mother by upholding the law. Conversely, we understand Sarah to be the spiritual union that is represented in "the Jerusalem that is above." The descendants of this free woman are those who are related to and are a part of the promised Seed of Abraham.

Paul painted this family portrait to illustrate how we come to our inheritance. Given what we have discovered from Abraham's story, would you rather be Isaac or Ishmael? Would you rather have a slave mother or a free mother? Would you prefer the closeness of family or separation? Do you desire an inheritance from your father? If you attempt righteousness through the law, you consequently are choosing the slave mother, separation, and exclusion from the inheritance. On the other hand, if you pursue righteousness by faith, you are choosing the free mother, inclusion in the family, and inheritance of the promise.

How Do I Get In on the Promise?

We have discussed at length what it means to be born of the slave woman, but how do we align ourselves with the free woman? We will devote the rest of this chapter to talking about how we become a part of the family and heirs along with Isaac. According to this teaching there are three distinct ways we achieve relationship.

1. We achieve relationship by faith.

As we discussed earlier in chapter four, Abraham was credited with righteousness and therefore free because of his faith. But faith is also what makes us sons of God. We know that God is righteous (see Ps 97:6), and we know that his Son is righteous (see Acts 7:52). Most families have something distinct about them. It could be anything from a physical feature like a big nose to the way they laugh or sneeze. You can often identify family members by common, distinctive traits. The defining trait of the family of God is righteousness. Therefore, those who are identified with this family will most resemble their father and their brother when they are righteous. And this righteousness comes by faith and is credited to us just as it was to Abraham. We have this wonderful promise that we become a part of the family by believing: "You are all sons of God through faith in Christ Jesus." The simple memory verse we teach children at an early age says it all, "Whoever believes in him shall not perish but have eternal life" (John 3:16). We are to understand that we will receive an inheritance of eternal freedom based on faith in Jesus alone.

2. We achieve relationship by belonging to Christ.

Believing in Jesus is the inward heart commitment, and baptism is the outward physical sign that represents several things: death, burial, and resurrection, being born again, having sins cleansed, and submission to Christ to name a few. But in these Scriptures Paul points out that baptism is a clothing of oneself with Jesus. This means that we take on traits of Jesus. When we are baptized into him, we begin to look like our older brother because we take on his spiritual qualities. We don't reach the perfection of Christ, but we love more, forgive more, serve more, and live more like our spiritual sibling. This clothing of Christ shows that we belong in his family. And the fact that he is the promised seed of Abraham means we are heirs according to the promise God made to the patriarch. No matter what others may say or how anyone may judge your lifestyle, if you have clothed yourself with Christ, you are identified with him and belong to him. This means you are entitled as a son or daughter to receive inheritance with him.

> **When we are baptized, we begin to look like our older brother.**

3. We achieve relationship by the power of the Holy Spirit.

There is another family member that we must mention before we end this discussion on relationship. The relationship we have with God through Jesus is made possible by the power of the Holy Spirit. Back to the original family of promise—the result of Sarah's pregnancy and delivery of Isaac was by supernatural power (see Gal 4:29). We previously mentioned that Ishmael was born in the ordinary way, but Isaac wasn't. Of course Abraham and Sarah must have had sexual relations, but the Spirit intervened to cause a ninety-year-old woman who was barren to be fruitful. Relationship with God, through Jesus, is achieved in the spiritual realm, not in the physical. This is why Paul tells the believers he is writing to that physical observance of the law will never get them in the family. In his mind it must be spiritual. Jesus taught the same thing about the Spirit when he told Nicodemus, "I tell you the truth, no one can enter the kingdom of God unless he is born of water and the Spirit. Flesh gives birth to flesh, but the Spirit gives birth to spirit" (John 3:5-6). By faith we are born into the spiritual family of God by the power of the Holy Spirit.

It should not be surprising to you that the entire Trinity is involved in securing the relationship of the believer. There is no family without a father (God). There is no way to take on family traits without clothing ourselves with our older brother (Jesus). And it is impossible to be born into a spiritual family by physical means; it must be by the power of the Holy Spirit.

Family membership has its privileges. We are free to live every day for Christ because we are sure to attain the eternal freedom that comes from being family members. Someday we will receive an inheritance based

> **Someday we will receive an inheritance based on our relationship.**

on the fact that we are related to the heavenly Father. And unlike the surprise inheritance I received from my grandfather, we can live in expectancy of this heavenly gift, for our Father is rich and our share is promised. [3:16]

6   *Freedom by Relationship*

Living Free

1. Spend time sharing with one another about your family. How many siblings were in your home? Blended family, traditional, adopted? How does your exact relationship within that family affect your status (were you an Isaac or an Ishmael)?

2. What privileges did you enjoy growing up as a result of being a part of the family?

3. What kind of inheritance do you expect your parents to leave you spiritually? Emotionally? Financially?

4. Have you ever been an heir? What did that feel like?

5. How would you live if you were guaranteed a million dollar inheritance from a rich relative upon their death? What would you do with such an inheritance?

6. How should you live considering God's guaranteed eternal inheritance? What is freeing about that?

Memory Verse
Gal 3:26-27

You are all sons of God through faith in Christ Jesus, [27]for all of you who were baptized into Christ have clothed yourselves with Christ.

CHAPTER SEVEN

FREEDOM OPPONENTS

GALATIANS 4:8-18

As I write this chapter, the sense of history making hangs in the air. The date is January 30, 2005, and nearly 60% of the Iraqi people are voting. It has been nearly two years since liberation from the dictatorial regime of Saddam Hussein, and now people from all over Iraq are freely making their way to highly secured polling stations to cast their ballots for candidates for the National Assembly. The images of grown men and women smiling, dancing, and celebrating fill the television screens. Why are they dancing? Many of these people have experienced the freedom of voting and voicing their opinion for the very first time in their lives. They proudly wait in long lines. They pore over the extensive ballot. They eagerly display their purple-stained index fingers—a telltale sign of their participation in the vote.

What makes this day of nationwide voting so remarkable is the danger that surrounds it. For months those opposing democracy and an elected government have struck terror in the hearts of everyone through car bombs, suicide bombers, and small arms fire. As the election day neared, they intensified their attacks and their threats. These terrorists had predicted a bloodbath on election day for those who persisted in voting. As a matter of fact, in spite of heavy security, at least forty suicide bombers (including one boy with Down's Syndrome) were successful in detonating themselves in or near several polling stations. As people celebrated this historical day of freedom, there were those who had dedicated themselves to doing everything in their power to prevent it. This is the irony of freedom movements throughout history. Wherever there is a chance at freedom, there will be those who try to prevent it. These people are freedom's opponents—those who war against the freedom opportunities of others.

> Wherever there is a chance at freedom, there will be those who try to prevent it.

Freedom opponents can also be found in the spiritual realm and in the kingdom of God. Jesus actually confronted a group of people during his ministry who were doing everything within their power to keep the people from being free. This group of leaders known as Pharisees were labeled by Jesus as "blind guides" (Matt 23:24). Though they had been entrusted with the teaching and direction of the people of Israel, they did not, in fact, know God and were no more effective than a guide who had no eyesight. Not only were they incapable of pointing people in the right direction, they were preventing people from finding freedom on their own. Jesus said of them, "They tie up heavy loads and put them on men's shoulders. . . . You shut the kingdom of heaven in men's faces. You yourselves do not enter, nor will you let those enter who are trying to" (Matt 23:4,13-14).

A couple of decades later, some Judaizers (probably some from the Pharisee sect mentioned above) were zealously fighting freedom among the Galatian Christians. They were passionately working for the cause of promoting the law and causing the Gentile believers to come close to God by the observance of rules. In reality, they were leading these young Christians away from the freedom they had found in Christ under Paul's tutelage. Paul says about them, "Those people are zealous to win you over, but for no good" (Gal 4:17). In this part of his letter to his "dear children," he warns them against giving in to those who oppose freedom.

Before reading the verses for this portion of our study, ponder for a moment those who fight against the freedom we have found in Christ today. Although we are not under the Pharisees' authority or leadership, there are certainly some pharisaical attitudes which creep into our churches. As you read, keep these two questions in mind: Am I a freedom opponent? Am I giving in to zealous freedom opponents around me?

Read Galatians 4:8-19 together as a group.

In this passage, Paul returns to the past that these believers had come from. He reminds them again that when he first met them, they were enslaved to gods who weren't gods at all. This is in reference to the many man-made gods and the worship that accompanied them throughout their region. But he goes a bit further here by comparing Judaism to paganism. Of course, he isn't talking about the worship of many gods. Judaism is monotheistic (believing in one God) and paganism is polytheistic (believing in many gods or deities). In fact, the God of the Jews is the God of Christianity. However, the celebration and observance of special days has many similarities.

The observance of special days is very much a part of most cultures. Most of us celebrate the day of our birth annually. This can be as simple as the exchanging of cards, or it may come complete with cakes, streamers, and presents. Most people celebrate anniversaries that mark special occasions. This is especially true of wedding anniversaries. Just about every day of the calendar has some significance attached to it. Special days abound.

The pagan culture of ancient Galatia had special or holy days (holidays) related to certain months and times of the year. Of course they worshiped gods, commonly called idols, fashioned by hand and made of precious metal and stone, but they also worshiped natural astral spirits like the sun, moon, and stars. They had a fascination for the galaxies, the unknown of outer space, and what they could not explain, so they worshiped these heavenly deities at certain times of the year like a full moon or when a new season approached.

The Jewish faith also celebrated holidays and special sacrifices outlined in the Old Testament according to seasons and days. This included feasts, Sabbath days and years, and holy days like Passover. What Paul is saying here is that the Jewish faith really resembles the pagan faith that the Galatians had been freed from. Those who were trying to convince them that they should follow the Jewish calendar to freedom were in actuality leading them back into the slavery of a pagan religion.

Paul cautions his readers that these teachers they are listening to are freedom opponents and that they are in fact turning back to slavery. This is why Paul asks in verse nine, "How is it that you are turning back to those weak and miserable principles?" In the remainder of this chapter we will look at three other questions asked in this section and use them to help determine if we are either fighting freedom or giving in to those who do.

"Do you wish to be enslaved by them all over again?" (Ritual vs. Relationship)

Those who are against freedom are for slavery. We can always identify freedom opponents by what they are promoting. Slavery will always promote ritual, and freedom will al- **Those who are against freedom are for slavery.** ways promote relationship. God is calling us to freedom. Freedom's opponents believe that the path to God can be obtained by ritual, but the gospel message declares that God desires relationship.

A close look at how a marriage works will illustrate our point. A marriage is an agreement for two people to spend their lives together in a loving relationship. The premise is that the woman and man involved both have a mutual love and desire for one another. But what if upon returning from the honeymoon, the husband presented his new bride with a list of things she needed to do in order to be his wife. On that list, there would be some sort of daily checklist: say "I love you" at least twenty times, kiss me every time I walk into the same room as you, lay out the clothes I will wear for the next day, etc.

For the sake of argument, if this woman complied with the wishes of her husband, and followed every one of the requirements on his list, would this be love? Even if we could define this as love on some level, would anyone you know be interested in having this kind of marriage arrangement? Is this marriage arrangement freeing or enslaving? What if on one particular day, the wife wanted to say "I love you" only nineteen times? Or add a kiss? Or prepare a nice dinner? Would this impromptu display of affection be acceptable? Not under the prescribed agreement. The only thing that would matter would be if every part of the agreement were followed to the letter. This is not a freeing situation.

A marriage works because two people commit to each other and grow in their love over time. As the honeymoon ends and the couple begins to work, pay bills, play, relax, laugh, disagree, etc., each begins to learn what pleases the other. Words of affection are spontaneous and meaningful. Kind acts are received as gifts. Apologizing in a sincere manner solidifies the love commitment. Working to accomplish the same goals becomes an adventure. Every day is filled with a variety of love expressions which makes the relationship interesting and fulfilling. This is the freedom of a loving relationship.

Paul tells us that we know God and are known by him—this is relationship. We are free to respond to him as his written word moves us, as his Spirit directs us, and as our individual experiences shape us. We can shout for joy or quietly kneel. We can praise him with any style of music. We can wear whatever clothing we want. We are free to live our lives in a variety of ways as an expression of relationship with God. The alternative is to go back to the law which gives us the requirements of relating to a holy God. We can follow all the commands and observe all

67

‡

C
H
A
P
T
E
R

7

the days, but in the end, our hearts may not truly love him. This is the slavery that many in Galatia were returning to.

Are you expecting someone to approach relationship with God under your terms? Are you telling him the right way to participate in the spiritual disciplines? Are you laying out terms for the right amount of prayer, the proper kind of worship, the more acceptable lifestyle? If so, you may be fighting the freedom in a fellow believer's life and actually damaging his relationship with God instead of enhancing it.

> **Are you expecting someone to approach relationship with God under your terms?**

The other caution is to live free and not let anyone else put his or her standards and requirements for relating to God on you. It is fine to have someone you look up to in the faith, but to mimic her personal relationship with God is not healthy. The beauty of relating to God is that each relationship is different. There are a lot of people who know me, but my sons, my wife, my mom, and my golf buddies all relate to me in very different ways. They can all claim relationship, but their experiences are vastly different. Relating to God is like that. We all know God, but each of us has a unique relationship with him. This leads to another revealing question about freedom.

> **The beauty of relating to God is that each relationship is different.**

"What has happened to all your joy?"
(Obligation vs. Joy)

Freedom opponents don't have time for joy. They are usually too stressed out trying to keep up with all the requirements to truly enjoy the presence of God in their lives. If you've been around church very long, you can identify those who are obligated to be there by their long faces and weary looks. Every bit of their daily walk is drudgery because they have to live this way. On the other hand, most congregations have those special few who light up the room when they enter. Smiles cover their face even when times are hard. An adventurous spirit emanates to those around them. Encouraging words flow from their mouths. These people are free to express joy.

A sure sign of a freedom opponent is that all the joy is gone. Paul recognized this in his Galatian brothers and sisters. Apparently the first visit to the region on the inaugural missionary journey was occasioned by Paul's illness. Paul and Barnabas had shared the gospel, and many had believed and were filled with joy. How joyful were these new con-

> **A sure sign of a freedom opponent is that all the joy is gone.**

verts? They were so elated that they would have given Paul their eyes to make him well if that would have been possible. These Christians had found freedom in Christ, and the physical didn't matter; they had found what was truly important.

Now Paul has received word that they are questioning his authority and teaching. Suddenly, they are not rejoicing in their salvation; they have turned critical and exclusive. Those who had once cared for the apostle during his illness were now rejecting him as their father in the faith. Paul could tell by their tone that they had lost their joy. This is a result of living in slavery.

In a later chapter we will discover that joy is a trait in Christians that evidences the Holy Spirit's presence. But for now, we can evaluate freedom opponents and freedom promoters by this simple attitude. Freedom's opponents consistently look for the bad in people, pointing out how immature they are in their faith. Those who promote freedom look for the positive growth in people. They are like old people at the family reunion who tell a four-year-old that they are "so big" even though they know there is so much growth ahead. Freedom opponents discourage by their standards. Freedom champions encourage with words of possibility. Freedom opponents sit in judgment on people who are not like them. Those who encourage freedom bring joy by their patience with weaker brothers and sisters.

Again, are you fighting freedom by seeing only the negative, speaking discouragingly, and sitting in judgment? Can your life be characterized as someone filled with joy, or do you steal it from others who might have it? Or perhaps, your spiritual joy has been quenched by someone in your church who has imposed his or her religious obligations on you. When pursuing freedom, always choose joy over obligation. This not only affects those within the church, but nonbelievers as well. When a lost world sees obligation and duty as the main motivation, they have no desire for such "freedom." However, if we can show them the joy that comes from knowing Jesus, they may be attracted to our Savior. Joy is contagious. This leads us to the third question.

"Have I become your enemy by telling you the truth?" (Deceit vs. Truth)

Beyond all else, the problem with freedom's opponents is that they are in the business of deceiving others for their gain. At the beginning of this chapter we observed Iraqi insurgents who threatened to kill anyone who voted. Their message is that the Americans are infidels who are defiling their land and their country by unlawfully promoting democracy. But the underlying motive behind this crusade isn't the truth of their message, rather the threat to their power. They opposed the vote because they knew that a free election would oust them from power. Their message was and is one of deceit to protect their place.

The Judaizers who had made their way to the cities of Galatia were motivated by their authority. If Christianity were to succeed, they would essentially be out of a job. If the law is no longer to be observed, then those who interpret and uphold the law would become unnecessary. Their zealous preaching to the Galatians was an attempt to convince them to follow the law and therefore their leadership. Paul simply claims to have told them the truth when he first came into their towns. His message was simple and did not bring him any personal gain. They accepted the truth then, and Paul is wondering if he is now their enemy because he is being honest with them.

Whenever another believer is trying to impose his faith's practices or standards on your life, it is important to try to discover his motives. There are many preachers who are motivated by keeping their jobs. There are some church leaders who are motivated to maintain power that they had for years. There are numerous church members who care only for their personal preferences. These people are freedom's opponents.

You can tell those in the church who want freedom by the truthfulness of their walk and their talk. These people are constantly searching the Scriptures to see what God considers right. They are willing to earnestly pray and seek God's will. These people will listen to and submit to other Christian brothers and sisters. These people are motivated by doing things the right way in God's eyes. They are seekers of the truth.

For the last time, are you fighting the freedoms of others in your local church because of a personal preference? Is there any biblical reason you can't compromise? Do you find yourself stretching the truth to strengthen your position? Or are you the victim of those more interested in their desires than knowing and living by the truth?

The vote in Iraq is another illustration of the human desire for freedom. Freedom will prevail. There will always be those who fight against it, but the desire for freedom is deeply embedded in each of us. May you and I be those who promote freedom, not fight against it, in the world and in the church. 3:16

Living Free

1. Are you expecting others to approach God on your terms and are thereby fighting the freedom God has bought for them?

2. What brings joy in your life as you walk with God?

3. What makes people lose the joy of the Lord? What or who has stolen some of your joy?

4. What can you do to bring joy into the lives of those around you?

5. How can your small group make your church a more joyful place?

6. What are some unhealthy motivations for people within the church? Are you guilty of some of them?

7. How can you gently get past these motivations to sincere serving?

Memory Verse
Gal 4:8-9

Formerly, when you did not know God, you were slaves to those who by nature are not gods. ⁹But now that you know God—or rather are known by God—how is it that you are turning back to those weak and miserable principles? Do you wish to be enslaved by them all over again?

CHAPTER EIGHT

A FREEDOM
PICTURE

GALATIANS 5:1-12

If you were a world-renowned artist who was commissioned to paint a picture of freedom, what would you paint? Not being an artist, I can only guess, but you'd probably begin with a freedom color—something bright to capture the essence of the idea. Freedom may be captured in the orange of a sunset. You may find it in the cool blue of the sea. The green of a rolling meadow or the red of a spring tulip may represent freedom best. Any of these vibrant colors would be a good place to start this painting. But colors alone wouldn't be enough to express freedom's grandeur. This picture would have to be worth a thousand words. It would have to symbolize it perfectly.

What visual would best illustrate freedom? A beautifully colored hot-air balloon certainly has the look of being unrestricted. A laughing child gliding through the air on a swing is a picture of the carefree. The wildness of an untamed mountain range would represent unexplored possibilities. A father dancing with his daughter on her wedding day is about life at its freest, happiest, and best. Flying the flag of your homeland represents the pride of your heritage. All of these would be worthy pictures to represent this incredible idea. Freedom is unrestricted, carefree, unexplored, and representative of where we came from, but what about spiritual freedom?

We have spent the bulk of this book discussing freedom's ring in the life of those who are in Christ. It has been helpful to discuss the significance of what the apostle was trying to say and to discover the truth of the word, but what does this free life really look like? Sure we are freed in Christ from the slavery of sin and the law, but how does that reality play itself out in the everyday life of the believer? If we could paint a picture of a Christian who was living in the freedom of Christ; what would that painting look like? This part of Paul's letter may give us some insight.

Before we read this passage, however, I want to draw attention to two instruments of rhetoric employed here by the author of Galatians. Paul was of course trained in the art of communication and speech. Having been the son of a Pharisee and on the fast track to success among young Jewish leaders, he would have been trained by the finest teachers of his time. He had command of languages and was well versed in the law. He may have also studied many of the world's philosophies, languages, and literature. He was an educated man who had a gift with words. Is it any wonder that God chose him to pen most of the New Testament?

In this section he uses sarcasm as the device to effectively make his point. One of the main issues for the Judaizers was that believers must be circumcised according to the law. Circumcision is cutting off the foreskin of the male anatomy and the word cut is woven into the teaching here. The readers of this letter may have found humor in this word structure (although it's hard to imagine that any Galatian male considered circumcision a humorous topic). He uses the word "cut" in verse seven as a play on words to describe the Galatians' abrupt, spiritual setback: "Who cut in on you and kept you from obeying the truth?"

Paul's ironic sense of humor also appears in verse twelve. We read that he had a wish for the male false teachers who had infiltrated the ranks of the Galatian churches. He challenges them to go the whole way and emasculate themselves. Again, circumcision dealt with cutting off the foreskin, but Paul was suggesting they go farther and become eunuchs! While this may have been considered humorous by first-century readers, they would definitely hear the apostle's serious message. Ironically, according to Old Testament law, any man who had his male genitalia removed would be "cut off" from the place of worshiping God (see Deut 23:1). Translation: Paul wants these false teachers totally cut off from God because of their enslaving message. Keep these ideas in mind as you read to better understand how the original recipients of this letter might have taken these words.

Read Galatians 5:1-12 together as a group.

We can see three noticeable images in this masterpiece called freedom. In keeping with our painting analogy, we'll examine each image

A Freedom Picture

in detail. Then we will explore its ramifications for our lives today. What does a picture of spiritual freedom look like?

An Oak Tree—Standing Firm

There is nothing more representative of standing firm than the proverbial mighty oak tree. It's the tree that many young homeowners plant in the front yard when the children are young. After many years, the grandchildren visit to play beneath its shade and the tree towers above the house itself. Over the years, tornadoes have blown by it, children have climbed it, and storms have shaken it; but it remains in place year after year, season after season. It remains because of its roots. The oak tree extends her roots deep for nutrients and stability. This is a picture of a believer who is free. There may be outside influences and a variety of circumstances, but because of deep roots, the Christian is able to stand firm.

Paul begins by reiterating that Christ died for the purpose of setting us free and then gives this first brush stroke at end of verse one: stand firm. If you were to ask Paul what Christian freedom looked like, he would paint a "standing firm" picture. A person who is free in Christ stands firm in his relationship with God, his faith in Christ, and the hope of his salvation. Freedom comes to those who know that no other relationship is more important than the one they have with God their Father. People of freedom understand that believing in the Son is more important than believing in right doctrines. Freedom is realized by those who hope for something better to come. Let's look at how we are to stand firm in these things.

> Freedom comes to those who know that no other relationship is more important than the one they have with God their Father.

You've probably heard someone say, "I don't care what other people think." People say this for many reasons. Some use this as a cop-out to do what they want because truthfully they are selfish and don't care about other people in general. Some make this statement in reference to specific people whose opinions don't matter because they don't respect them or have relationship with them. Still others use this phrase because they are very independent and able to live life without the approval of others.

Whatever the case, not caring what other people think is part of the firm foundation upon which Christians must plant themselves. The only one Christians ultimately must please is God. There is freedom in knowing that life is simply an exercise in pleasing God. If my relationship with God is in place, then no other opinion really matters. This is the sentiment already expressed in this letter earlier: "As for those who seemed to be important—whatever they were makes no difference to me; God does not judge

by external appearance—those men added nothing to my message." (Gal 2:6). You may recall that Paul was meeting the Jerusalem leaders for the first time and was a bit apprehensive, but you will see by this statement he was standing firm in ministry because of his calling by God and not their endorsement. In a sense, he didn't care what others (even major apostles) thought of his ministry. He was pleasing God. This was in fact Paul's goal in life (see 2 Cor 5:9), and it should be that of every believer.

Paul encouraged these Galatians to stand firm in their relationship with God and not give in to pleasing these teachers who had infiltrated their ranks. These baby Christians had gone from a life of pleasing God to one of pleasing these Jewish teachers. They were submitting to circumcision and Jewish rituals in order to make these people happy. This is not freedom.

The word for today's followers is that we are called to the freedom of pleasing God and him alone. As a pastor, there have been many people over the years who would have preferred that I do ministry a different way. At times I have been tempted to please them—to give in to their desires—simply to make them happy. But I have found in the long run that after much prayer, seeking godly advice, studying the Word, and following the Spirit's leading, it serves me best to follow the path I feel God is leading me down. Some people don't like it, but in the end, I can't worry about pleasing them.

Christians are often tempted to try to live up to the standards of those who attend the same church, are involved in the same group, or work together in the same ministry. Some have been made to feel guilty about schooling their children (home, Christian, or public school), movies they watch (to "R" or not to "R"), Bible studies (the more, the holier), appearance (hair, makeup, and clothes), service (soup kitchens, mission trips, local charities), and many more. While all of these are subject to personal freedom, many try to make them tests of faith and salvation. People who are free stand firm in the privilege of choosing how to live out their faith. True Christians find freedom in knowing God, talking with him, studying his Word, following his Spirit and standing firm.

Christians are also encouraged in this passage to stand firm in their faith in Christ. He is the one who set us free. You can't be free and turn your back on the Savior, the one who gave you freedom. Again, this narrows the things we must believe down to one. We must believe that Jesus Christ is both Savior and Lord. Jesus said to Martha, "I am the resurrection and the life. He who believes in me will live, even though he dies; and whoever lives and believes in me will never die" (John 11:26). Later this disciple who recorded these words would encourage his readers: "Everyone who believes that Jesus is the Christ is born of God" (1 John 5:1). We can find a firm foundation in our faith in Christ.

You may think this is a strange point to make. "After all," you may ask, "doesn't every Christian know that believing in Jesus is the point to Christianity?" Often you will find someone professing faith in Jesus verbally, but in reality they are placing their faith in other things as well. There is at least a possibility that these Jewish teachers in Galatia believed in Jesus as Messiah, but they also believed in the law and its teachings. They were calling believers to acknowledge that circumcision, fasts, ritual prayers, and sacrifices were items of faith as well. Paul points out: "If you let yourselves be circumcised, Christ will be of no value to you at all" (Gal 5:2). He knows that the moment they place their faith in an act (circumcision), they will lose faith in their Lord (Jesus). This is not freedom.

In our day few are being pressured to be circumcised, but there are other manifestations of this faith shift. Some are pressured to follow denominational guidelines. Many today feel guilty for not worshiping and serving in the church of their heritage, guilt brought on by comments from parents and church leaders. Some are pressured to believe in certain doctrines that may include everything from eschatological positions to how we should administer the sacraments. Still others are pressured to believe that certain styles of worship are more holy or reverent and are actually made to feel unspiritual for not complying with these styles.

You are called to be free. If you place your faith in a denomination or church, you have jeopardized your standing with Christ. If you put faith in having knowledge and understanding of "right theology," you may jeopardize your freedom in him. If you give in to a form of worship or faith, you may miss the point. Jesus simply calls us to believe in him. This means that we seek to please him because he is Lord and we trust our souls to him because he is Savior. There is nothing else to believe. You can stand firm in this kind of faith.

Finally, Christians are called to stand firm in their future. We will not elaborate on this point here because it coincides with our second picture of "eager expectation." However, notice quickly in verse five of our reading that Paul talks about a hope. This is one of the hallmarks of the Christian faith. We are free because we have hope. This hope comes from relationship with God by faith in Christ. It is sure and it changes how we live. Those false teachers in Galatia were casting doubt on their eternity with God, but Paul encourages them about the righteousness for which they hope. This is another place Christians can find sure footing. But standing firm is only part of this freedom picture.

A Child on Christmas Eve—Eager Expectation

Part of the freedom experience in Christ is the anticipation that the life we now live by faith is only the beginning; there is something better ahead. To understand this Christian idea we might paint a picture of a little child on Christmas Eve. For weeks, presents have multiplied under the tree, each wrapped in brightly colored paper and bows. The stories of sugar plums, reindeer, and baby Jesus have filled the imagination of every child's mind. Now with the reflection of Christmas lights on the bedroom ceiling, Mom and Dad tuck the little ones in with a prayer. Tomorrow is Christmas. The anticipation of that day is overwhelming. All children have great expectations of many toys, and they can't wait until they are allowed to open them up. This kind of eager anticipation is the second brush stroke of the apostle's picture of freedom.

Paul says in this teaching that we are eagerly awaiting something. What is it that Christians are waiting for? Righteousness. On one hand, the Judaizers were teaching that the Galatians would only attain righteousness by following the rules. On the other hand, Paul taught that our righteousness would come to us by the Holy Spirit in the future. One is freedom, the other is not.

Under the law, people knew that they were sinners. They were reminded annually of this truth and were called to sacrifice and follow the commandments in pursuit of forgiveness. This means that everyday life became the tedious chore of watching every word and action and living with a constant realization of failure. The gospel also begins with an admission of our guilt, but it provides a Savior to completely forgive. This means that everyday life is lived knowing that all sins have been completely washed away. This allows the everyday life of the believer to focus solely on living for God and not on whether or not one is worthy. Our worthiness is found in our promised future righteousness.

Not unlike a child anticipating the gifts on Christmas morning, we look forward to unwrapping what we will become eternally. We know that the gift is ours, but we won't fully experience it until that day when Jesus comes to take us home. And so we anxiously await that transformation. Then and only then, can we truly live in the freedom that Christ has given us. When we know we are destined to be righteous, it allows us to focus on loving and honoring God with all of our life. And when we know that our hope is in the future, we can learn to place our hope in the eternal instead of the earthly. Paul writes to the Christians in Colosse: "Set your minds on things above, not on earthly things. For you died, and your life is now hidden with Christ in God" (Col 3:2-3).

A Marathon Runner—Running Well

I've always been intrigued by marathon runners. It's not the winning that really matters in a race that spans over 26 miles. What matters is overcoming. Only a few will actually have the athleticism and mental toughness it takes to win a marathon, but literally millions of people have competed. If you have ever seen a marathon runner cross the finish line, you have witnessed freedom. Exhaustion and fatigue give way to elation and accomplishment as the athlete celebrates victory over the distance and the constant desire to quit. It doesn't matter that they didn't finish in the top 5,000. What matters is that they worked and sweat and bled and kept going. The training paid off. The goal was accomplished.

The final image in this freedom picture comes from the sports world. Much like the culture in which we live, the first-century world was obsessed with sports. Most major cities had arenas that featured such major sporting events as chariot races, wrestling, running, and gladiatorial fights. Taking advantage of this phenomenon, Paul uses a sports image here to describe what the false teachers were doing to the Galatian believers in a spiritual sense. He writes in verse seven that though they were running a good race, someone had cut in on them.

Distance runners will tell you that there is some strategy to running a race of such length. There comes a time in each race where a competitor decides to challenge someone ahead of them. This often includes a quick burst of speed around the opponent and a cutting in front of them. This is mentally devastating. The visual of being passed and cut in front of, causes most runners to despair and feel tired, which gives way to discouragement and slowing. As the opponent cuts in and increases speed, the passed runner tends to slow, making the pass even more dramatic. The only way to defeat this tactic is to keep a steady pace and maintain proper running form. At this point, you must let your opponent affect your race as little as possible. Speeding up to keep up with them may deplete your energy for the long haul. Falling back too far may cause discouragement and cause you to run slower than you are capable of.

The people who had received Paul's original freedom message were running a good race, until the false teachers passed them with their law-driven religion. This had slowed the Galatians' pace for God and brought discouragement and spiritual defeat. Unfortunately, these "cutters" (again circumcision irony) had caused the Galatians to slow due to the weight of following the law. They had caused them to veer off course by taking their focus off of the gospel (". . . kept you from obeying the truth"). In short, the Galatians were not running freely.

If you are running for God, chances are you will experience those who cut in. Nehemiah experienced it when he was rebuilding the wall of Jerusalem. Noah experienced it when he was building an ark in the middle of a desert. Moses experienced it when he was leading God's people from Egypt to the Promised Land. Jesus experienced it from the spiritual leaders of the first century as he came to save the world. You and I can be distracted from living the Christian life, from running the race we began. In your walk (or run) of faith there will be those who detract, criticize, discourage, gossip, lie, and envy. The key is to keep your focus on Christ and run to the best of your ability so that you can finish. This probably sounds familiar: "But one thing I do: Forgetting what is behind and straining toward what is ahead, I press on toward the goal to win the prize for which God has called me heavenward in Christ Jesus" (Phil 3:13-14).

With the help of the apostle and some imagination, our freedom picture is complete. To live in the freedom of Jesus, we as Christians should stand firm as an oak tree; planted on the firm foundation of our faith, we should anticipate our future like a child on Christmas Eve; and we should run a good race focused on the prize.

Living Free

1. Pass out sheets of paper and pencils to each group member as your group time begins. Give ten minutes for each to draw a picture of freedom. Have each person show and explain their drawings.

2. Make a list of things you know about your faith. These are the things you stand firm on.

3. Make a list of things you look forward to the most about eternal promises of God. Include a favorite Scripture or promise that means the most to you. These are the things you eagerly expect.

4. Make a list of the things that have a tendency to cut in on your race of faith.

5. What things do you need to focus on spiritually in order to run a better race?

Memory Verse
Gal 5:6

For in Christ Jesus neither circumcision nor uncircumcision has any value. The only thing that counts is faith expressing itself through love.

CHAPTER NINE

FREEDOM BY THE SPIRIT

GALATIANS 5:16-26

The Old Testament records a strange provision for servants and masters. Both Exodus 21:2-6 and Deuteronomy 15:12-18 give instructions for the servant who is granted freedom, but chooses to remain a slave. It seems unbelievable that a slave would refuse the chance to go free, but apparently there were circumstances in which a slave would choose to submit to one he trusted and loved. Could it be that someone could find true freedom while in full submission?

Every six years, the people of God were instructed to release all of their Hebrew slaves. On the first day of the seventh year, the owner would come to the slaves' quarters and say, "Today is your day of freedom. You have been faithful and served me well for six years, but now by law you are free to go. Go in peace." I can't imagine this would have been some kind of surprise to the servant. Undoubtedly, he had spent many days thinking about the moment that he would be able to live on his own again, literally counting the days until freedom. Many probably had their belongings packed and ready to go. As a matter of fact, the masters were instructed to supply their newly emancipated brothers with grain, flocks, and wine (see Deut 15:14). This would get them started in their new life of freedom. At this point, it would have been normal for the slave to accept the gifts, pack his belongings, and journey home to his family with a fresh start. It would not be normal to ask to remain a slave!

Yet there was a provision made in the law whereby the slave could announce to his master that he did not want to leave. In some circumstances the servant may have learned to love his master because of his kindness. The slave may have considered the possibilities of freedom and concluded that he was better off remaining in servitude. In this case, the servant could appeal to his master to stay. This led to a ceremony that would designate the man a servant for life. The master would take the man to the door of his house and drive a nail through his ear lobe. This would mark him with an earring that would identify him as belonging to his master. Perhaps this is what David was alluding to in Psalm 40:6 when he said, "Sacrifice and offering you did not desire, but my ears you have pierced."

The Christian walk of freedom is very much like a slave who desires to be free by choosing to remain a servant. Truly, freedom is the ability to choose whom you will serve. In this portion of the Galatian letter,

> **Freedom is the ability to choose whom you will serve.**

the apostle talks of two masters who war within us competing for our allegiance. One is the sinful nature and the other is the Spirit of God. In these verses Paul encourages the believers to find freedom by giving complete control of their lives to the Holy Spirit.

Read Galatians 5:16-25 together as a group.

Did you notice the words that call us to submit to the Holy Spirit's leading in this passage? We are encouraged to live by the Spirit (v. 16), be led by the Spirit (v. 18), and to keep in step with the Spirit (v. 25). The true path to freedom is allowing ourselves to be mastered by the Holy Spirit. Like a servant, we are called to live every day in consideration of this Master. We are instructed to follow every leading of this trusted Owner. We are encouraged to imitate every step he takes as he guides us through life. But before we can be free by choosing servanthood to the Spirit, we must first reject slavery to the things of the world. Paul gives us a clear view of two masters and the results of slavery to each. The one we choose to serve will determine whether we live a life of freedom or slavery.

The Road to Slavery

Imagine if the slave misjudged the character of the master he had worked under. What would happen if after a few years of lifetime service, this formerly kind and considerate owner became a tyrant? What if the owner were in reality mean and selfish and cruel to his servants? What if servanthood became daily beatings, degrading comments, and unmet needs? In this case, the servant who had chosen a lifetime of slavery would find himself in the worst kind of slavery of all—the kind that never ends. What appeared to be freedom would become a hopeless and futile existence until the relief of death. This is the servant who becomes a lifelong slave to the master called sinful nature!

The apostle compiles a pretty extensive list of acts related to the sinful nature. It is important to note that these things are in war against the Spirit, actually competing for our allegiance. Notice that all fifteen of these obvious signs that enslave us to the sinful nature are acts. These are things people do to demonstrate who their master is. Even though there are fifteen individual acts, they can be broken down into four major categories.

Sexual Sins

As we have discussed, the Galatian province was filled with all kinds of sexual immorality. This would be defined as any sex act that occurs outside of the holy commitment between a man and woman called marriage. The apostle would go on to list "impurity" and "debauchery" which relate to perverted or violent sexual acts. "Orgies" obviously describes group sex. Much of what he is describing is the sexually driven worship of false gods in these cities. It also describes much of the world in which we live. From the beach to music videos to Victoria's Secret specials to pornography, our society is saturated with sexual images. Unfortunately, most of the free sexuality promoted in our world today is terribly enslaving. The draw of sexual temptation takes advantage of our God-given sexuality, and seems like a desirable master, but the results speak for themselves. This master has left too many people with broken marriages, guilt, sexually transmitted diseases, tattered hearts, unwanted pregnancies, lost innocence, and out-of-control lifestyles. Is this freedom?

Idolatry

A major part of the Galatian culture was wrapped up in worshiping false gods. Most of these were idols erected in various temples in each town. These people actually bowed down and worshiped images carved out of precious metals and stones. We could easily associate witchcraft with idolatry since it is the worship of something other than the true God. While most of us will never bow down to an idol or practice witchcraft, we are still at risk for idolatry. The materialistic world that we live in causes us to worship money and the things money can buy. It is an alluring master promising both happiness and contentment. But in the end this master enslaves us in a never-ending cycle of wanting more and never having enough. Do free people feel compelled to accumulate possessions?

Hurting Others

Another component of this master of the flesh is actions that are harmful to other people. The flesh enslaves us with hatred for those who have hurt us or are just not like us. We are handcuffed by being jealous of something another has. Human beings are tempted to huddle with those like them and damage the reputation of outsiders. Many times we are tempted to think only of ourselves, living a life of complete selfishness. Whether it's America or Galatia, people often do and say harmful things to others. But this too is a master that turns on us. People who, in the name of freedom, walk all over everyone else to get what they want will eventually end up without anyone in their lives. This leads to a double curse—slavery and loneliness.

Drunkenness

The final attribute of slavery to the sinful nature is that of being drunk. This is the devastating condition of drinking so much alcohol as to lose complete control of motor skills, speech, and judgment. There is an allure to numbing yourself to the pain of life or to being the life of the party. However, hangovers, drunk-driving accidents, and embarrassing actions follow this behavioral pattern. What seems to be a master that brings freedom actually ends up taking total control and often costing the person more than they wanted to pay.

Paul lists fifteen actions that seem to be freedom, yet lead to slavery. These are the things we are often drawn to because of our human (sinful) nature, yet there is another master who waits to take control and lead us to freedom. He is the Holy Spirit, and it is in choosing to be pierced by him that we gain a lifetime of freedom. To contrast the actions of the flesh, Paul lists the fruit of the Holy Spirit living within us. There are nine attributes that he points out that those who have chosen to walk by the Spirit display. It is important to note a couple of points here before we proceed. First, these are not separate fruits. If the Spirit lives inside of us, this is the fruit we will eventually bear. The idea is not to try to take on love or joy or peace but to yield more and more to the Spirit so that all of these things shine forth. Second, this is not a list of things you do. The lists of the flesh were actions, but the fruit of the Holy Spirit is evidence that a life has been given over to the control of the Spirit. You don't "do" this fruit, you become.

The Way of Submission

As we list the fruit that the Spirit is growing in each of our lives, we will categorize some of them together and contrast them with the acts of the sinful nature. This will display clearly the difference between two masters who are calling us to serve them.

Love

The first part of the Spirit's fruit is love. This should not surprise us since God is love and to understand love is to know Him. This is not just any kind of love however. It is one of four Greek words for love. The word "agape" is a love with no conditions on it. This love of God cares for someone regardless of his ability to pay that person back. When the Holy Spirit takes control of the believer's life, a selfless love will flow towards those who can't repay love. A Christian teenager will find the ability to sit with, hug, and care for that mentally handicapped student that the other teenagers make fun of. Christian adults will use their house to entertain those who never get invited and feel left out. The lonely, outcast, homeless, helpless, and hapless will stir compassion in the hearts of the Spirit-filled Christian and move them to action. This is in direct contrast to the "love" that the world offers. Those who bear Holy Spirit fruit don't engage in the sexual imitation of love, they learn to truly love like their Father.

> When the Holy Spirit takes control of the believer's life, a selfless love will flow towards those who can't repay love.

Joy

The world searches for happiness and the euphoria that comes from the next party or special event, but the Spirit instills deep-down contentment regardless of the situation. The influence of the Holy Spirit allows Christians to have a steady emotional outlook even when the worldly perspective is bleak. Christian joy is the smile on the face of the pastor as he listens to the testimony of a changed life that he influenced. Joy manifests itself in a worship song during a funeral service as tears mingle with a smile. Joy is able to find beauty in every moment of life. To followers of Christ, even something as mundane as changing diapers, mowing the lawn, or enjoying an ice cream cone can be a joyful occasion.

> The Spirit instills deep-down contentment regardless of the situation.

Peace

This word is mentioned in the New Testament over 37 times. As in most letters, Paul introduces this letter by bestowing peace on his readers. Now he teaches that peace is part of the Holy Spirit's work in our lives. Peace is close to joy because it too is a contentment word, but it is contentment in the knowledge that God is in control. Peace is calm in the storm and determination in the face of the unknown. When a Christian gets laid off suddenly, there is a peace that comes from the Spirit. When there is family turmoil with no solutions or answers in sight, a believer can pray and receive an unexplainable peace that God is in control. People who follow the Spirit can sleep at night even though they are moving to a new place where they don't know anyone. The Spirit brings peace.

Patience

In an instant gratification culture, when this attribute comes to fruition, it is noticeable. This may be some of the most difficult growing most Christians do. Patience is the ability to wait on God's timing because we trust his perspective and his plan. Many times life is frustrating because we want to know what is next. How will our kids grow up? Will my marriage be successful? Will I get married? What purpose does God have for my life? When will this dream come true? These and many other questions of timing fill our minds, but the Spirit works in us to wait upon the Lord. The Holy Spirit forges patience in the heart of the young woman who wants to be a wife and mom but isn't even dating. The Spirit causes the person who was passed over for promotion to wait for next time. The believer who desires to become a world-renowned artist using the gift God has given to the glory of his name displays the spiritual attribute of patience when he continues to serve and use his gift in less glamorous settings.

Joy, peace, and patience can be seen as a group and contrasted to the idolatry of the world. Whereas the world is dependent on possessions and parties for happiness, the spiritual person finds joy in every day and every thing. Peace that God is in charge escapes those who live by the flesh, for when their gods don't bring happiness, their phoniness is revealed. In the same way, the world cannot be patient because there is no promise that the future will be any better, yet the believer can wait because eventually God's will will triumph in the end. It is obvious that the way to freedom is following the contentment of joy, peace, and patience.

> The world cannot be patient because there is no promise that the future will be any better.

Kindness

Kindness is the outward action of the inward love discussed above. It is an action that benefits someone else or meets one of their needs.

"You are special" and other words of kindness reveal Holy Spirit work in the life of the believer. Holding the door can be a Christian act. Allowing someone to cut in front of you at the grocery store or in traffic may display a kind heart. Kindness can also be pushing a wheelchair or holding the umbrella as you escort an elderly person indoors. When you see someone doing something kind for another, you may be seeing fruit from the Spirit of God.

Goodness

This word can be defined as doing the right thing all of the time. You have heard someone described as having "a good heart." This is an indication that their actions are pure, always in line with God's standard of right and wrong. This causes the person controlled by the Spirit to pay the government all of their taxes. Goodness always tells the truth (it doesn't allow for even "little white lies"). A Christian displaying goodness would never steal a towel from a hotel or eat grapes they never intend to pay for at the grocery store. The believer who lives by goodness works hard at the place of her employment (even when the boss isn't around). The goodness of the Spirit manifests itself in giving the biggest piece of pie to a friend.

Faithfulness

In a world where people quit on marriage, give up on friends, and walk away from hard work, faithfulness is a sharp contrast. To be faithful is to be there no matter what. Faithfulness is dependability. One who is faithful is an authentic person who gives her word and means it. The faithful claim Jesus as Lord and then live their lives as though he is in charge. A Christian can be faithful by standing up for a friend who is under criticism. Faithfulness can be found in the life of a believer who could walk away from a difficult marriage but is committed to see it through. You can see faithfulness in the life of the 80-year-old believer who never misses an opportunity to worship with the church every weekend.

Gentleness

My mother used to refer to me when I was roughhousing as a "bull in a China shop." Gentleness is the opposite of that. The gentle spirit is unassuming. Someone who is gentle is quiet. The gentleness that the Spirit grows in each of us is not overpowering. "Meek" is a word that describes our Lord, and his Spirit teaches us to be like him. Gentle is a former football lineman rocking a baby. A Christian father wrestling with his two-year-old is gentle. A wise pastor, who listens to the ranting of a disgruntled member and responds with thoughtful insight, is gentleness in action.

Again we pause to compare the acts of the sinful nature to the fruit of the Spirit. The Spirit leads us to be kind, good, faithful, and gentle towards others. This is the opposite of jealousy, selfishness, envy, and the like. The fruit of the Spirit brings freedom in relationships with others.

> **The fruit of the Spirit brings freedom in relationships with others.**

Self-control

This word literally means to "have in hand your passions and desires." I picture a large remote control. The buttons I push dictate my words, my actions, and my thoughts. With the help of the Holy Spirit, the Christian never relinquishes control of himself. This again is in contrast with the flesh. Drunkenness is being controlled by alcohol in the bloodstream; self-control is being influenced by another kind of Spirit.

Paul gives a command concerning these two in Ephesians 5:18: "Do not get drunk on wine, which leads to debauchery. Instead, be filled with the Spirit." Because the believer yields to the Spirit's fruit growing inside, he will not let his tongue fly or his actions precede his thinking. The man or woman of God will work at controlling who they are with the Spirit's guidance and help.

Could it be that we can find true freedom by being in full submission? The apostle is telling the Galatians and us that choosing to remain in the lifetime service of the Spirit is in fact freedom. 3:16

Living Free

1. Have you ever felt the Holy Spirit distinctly move in your life? What happened?

2. What fruit of the Holy Spirit is most evident in your life? Why?

3. What fruit of the Holy Spirit is least evident in your life? Why?

4. What fruit of the Holy Spirit do you desire to exhibit more in your life?

5. Have each group member share with the others the fruit they see in each other.

6. Pray to God as a group, recommitting to voluntarily submitting to the Holy Spirit.

| **Memory Verse** Gal 5:22-23 | *But the fruit of the Spirit is love, joy, peace, patience, kindness, goodness, faithfulness, [23]gentleness and self-control. Against such things there is no law.* |

CHAPTER TEN

FREEDOM TO SERVE

GALATIANS 6:1-10

In his now famous *A Treatise on Christian Liberty* the reformer Martin Luther sets forth two propositions concerning the freedom that we have in Christ and how it relates to serving: "A Christian man is perfectly free, lord of all, subject to none. A Christian man is a perfectly dutiful servant of all, subject to all."[1] These two statements sum up the apostle's sentiment in this section of his letter as he teaches further on the purpose for our freedom. In an incredible paradox, we are free from the oppression of all people, and yet we are called to serve all people. In this chapter we will discuss how our freedom allows us to serve.

Many people believe the idea of Christian freedom gives them the license to do whatever they want. Some believers are even tempted to use this freedom to indulge in the sinful nature. I know Christians who swear regularly and seem to make no effort to stop. Some Christians turn to alcoholic drink and push right to the edge of being influenced by its effects. Most Christ-followers have no qualms about eating way beyond their capacity and show no constraint in their diets. There are some believers who watch raunchy television shows and listen to music with more bleeps than words. There are some Christian women who wear provocative clothing. Some Christians get together and regularly cross the line of appropriate dialogue concerning sexuality. Does our freedom allow such actions and expres-

> Some believers are even tempted to use this freedom to indulge in the sinful nature.

sions? Are Christians free or not? Of course they are, but we must ask ourselves if we were set free so that we could literally do any earthly thing we desire. Did Christ die so that you and I could do as we please? Simply, no. Christ gave us freedom for so much more than doing what we want. In fact the best expressions of freedom are found in submission. In the last chapter we learned that we find freedom in submitting to the Holy Spirit and in this chapter we learn that we can also be free by learning to serve one another.

Read Galatians 5:13-15 together as a group.

As we have discussed from the beginning of this book, the apostle argues adamantly that we have been freed from the law, yet even the law makes provision for freedom. Most of the law was designed to take care of the needs of others. By observing the command not to commit adultery, the needs of intimacy and trust between spouses was protected. The law not to steal assured everyone that their possessions were safe. Not bearing false witness allowed people to be spoken of truthfully. Obviously, "thou shall not murder" was put in place to preserve and protect everyone who belonged to the holy community. This is why the apostle says in Galatians 5:14 that the whole law could be "summed up in a single command: 'Love your neighbor as yourself.'" This powerful truth echoes Christ's words in Matthew 22:37-40 (both are quoting Lev 19:18). We have discussed at length how the law was part of what we have been freed from in Christ. But if the law is about serving others, then how much more must the message of freedom be about serving? In fact, this was Paul's ministry philosophy. In 1 Corinthians 9:19 he says, "Though I am free and belong to no man, I make myself a slave to everyone, to win as many as possible."

Before we go further into our study and learn exactly how our freedom encourages us to serve others, let's consider one attitude shift necessary to make it happen. We find the attitude that Paul advocates for true servants in Galatians 6:3. There Paul says, "If anyone thinks he is something when he is nothing, he deceives himself." We can only learn to serve other people by changing the way we look at ourselves and, in turn, those around us. Many times we deceive ourselves by having a pretty lofty view of who we are. Many times we reason that our sins are not as bad as those people we go to church with. Or we may believe that by virtue of our upbringing we have more class. Some tend to think they are better because they make more money or have been more successful than others.

In order to serve others, these high-minded attitudes have to change. The apostle teaches that anyone who thinks he has his act

> **The only way to become a servant of others is to see people differently.**

together is not being honest with himself. He has forgotten the bondage that once held him. Christians sometimes forget that Jesus gained a freedom for them that they could never attain on their own. They have forgotten that those they look down on are a reflection of who they once were. The only way to become a servant of others is to see people differently.

When you see a homeless person walking toward you, what do you think? When you think of people at a party drinking until they can't stand up, what emotion fills your heart? When you see a dirty kid in tattered clothes playing in the street, what feelings do you have? When you learn that someone in your church has been divorced, where do you place them on the righteousness scale? When you meet someone who is a practicing homosexual, how does your demeanor change? When you see teenagers smoking in a back alley, do you care more about them or the cigarette? These are difficult questions, but they illustrate how often and easily we categorize people. In order to serve, we must not place them beneath us, we must stand beside them. Only the recognition that we are not better than they will allow us to serve like Christ.

Read Galatians 6:1-10 together as a group.

Serving others can be extremely tiring. It's not easy to do good for others. One cannot work in a nursing home without working extremely hard to meet the needs of the patients. The repetitive duties of changing, feeding, and caring for the elderly and medically challenged in this setting would wear most people out. Working in a day-care center for preschool children is also labor intensive. Countless trips to the bathroom, picking up toys, and periodic snack times exhaust even the most energetic worker. Being a mom is a role that calls for serving. Laundry, carpooling, cooking, cleaning, and shopping are just the beginning of the work list many women have for taking care of their families.

Many of us couldn't or wouldn't perform many of the tasks mentioned above, but that doesn't excuse us from hard work for others. The apostle Paul encourages his readers in Galatia to use their freedom to serve. In his mind, a Christian is called to be a servant; someone who does good things for others. He knows that sometimes we will get tired. That's why he says not to become "weary in doing good" (Gal 6:9). Let's look now at how God has set us free to serve others. In this part of our study, we will find four expectations for service.

Serve Those Who Sin (6:1)

This is a labor of love. Dealing with people who have been caught in sin is a service of a spiritual kind. It may not be physically exhausting, but it can be overwhelming emotionally. We are called to do good to others by restoring to the grace and love of Jesus a brother or sister who has sinned. The word "caught" in this verse is not the word that means "to be found out." This is not "caught red-handed" or "caught with their hand in the cookie jar." Sadly, there have been several occasions throughout my ministry career when someone in our congregation was "caught" in an adulterous relationship. This usually means that the illicit relationship becomes public knowledge. This is usually a devastating experience for all parties involved as well as the local body. Sooner or later most sins are exposed, but this is not what Paul is talking about when someone is caught in sin.

The word he uses here indicates entrapment. Picture a frustrated and angry animal that has stepped into a hunter's trap and now dangles overhead in a huge net, struggling to set itself free. The actions of this animal have caused it to be caught in the snare of the trapper. This is the picture the apostle wants believers to see when a brother or sister is involved in sinful actions. In this instance we are called to serve them because of our freedom.

The first part of this service to our fellow family member is to notice. Sometimes Christians are like parents in denial. We may see the signs of pride, hear the conversation of lust, detect the dishonesty, or smell the alcohol, but we choose to look the other way. To serve others we have to pay close attention to the walk of faith those around us are engaged in. This is not an invitation to impose our beliefs on others and become the freedom opponents described in chapter 7. This is an awareness of one of God's children violating his ways. We are called to serve by holding each other accountable to the Word of God. Many try to brush the sins of others aside arguing that it's "none of my business." This kind of attitude ignores the answer to the question Cain asked God in Genesis 4:9: "Am I my brother's keeper?" The answer for Cain and for us is "yes." We are called to keep an eye out for those who have been trapped by sin.

Noticing the fact that others are caught in sin is not enough. We are also called to deal with them gently. Some things in life require gentleness. A brain surgeon should be gentle. A nursery worker should be gentle. A jeweler must be gentle for the intricacies of the

> We are called to serve by holding each other accountable but we must be gentle.

job. And a Christian who is serving someone caught in sin must be gentle. Returning to the trapped animal picture, a person trapped by sin, like the animal, may be angry, hurt, scared, and aggressive. It doesn't matter that you are right in confronting this person; he or she may react in any or all of the above ways. The key is to be gentle.

The first thing we must try to do with people who are caught is to assure them that we are there to help instead of hurt. Paying attention to the pain they are in is a good place to start. Even though it is often of their own doing, most people who are living in sin are hurting emotionally, spiritually, and even physically. The best first step is to assure them that in spite of their sin you will be with them and that you love them and that God loves them.

Second, we must ask questions to help them verbalize how they got to where they are and why they are living as they are. The Holy Spirit will guide us in gentleness here. Remember part of his fruit in us is gentleness. Pray for him to help you ask the right spiritual questions without being too harsh. The best rule is, if you are unsure, just remain silent. Your presence will speak volumes and they will eventually talk. I've sat quietly with people for up to thirty minutes. Of course, most of us aren't trained to get to the bottom of people emotionally and spiritually. A gentle encouragement to seek Christian counseling is always a good idea.

Remember to show gentleness with your body language. If they are angry, don't allow yourself to be drawn into an argument. Simply remain calm and maintain a stance that is inviting. Usually a hug, a hand on the shoulder, a quiet demeanor, and a listening heart are enough to tenderize their hearts. Speak softly or not at all. Listening can be so powerful. Just continually remind yourself that you are representing Christ in this situation. Picture your Lord gently speaking with the woman caught in adultery, tenderly touching the blind man's eyes, and crying with Mary and Martha. Imitate the Master in this situation.

Finally, we serve those who sin by remembering we are not there to condemn them, but to restore them. We are there to remind them of the freedom found in the forgiveness of Jesus. They may have gotten drunk, committed adultery, lived a life of deceit or theft, but if they are in Christ, he offers complete forgiveness. Not only are we called to offer forgiveness, but restoration. Again, this begins with God's work in their lives. This is where the service gets hard. You may need to offer your time, listening ear, and maybe your resources to help them repair the devastation that often follows sinful practices. My favorite verse in serving those caught in sin is 1 John 1:9: "If we confess our sins, he is faithful and just and will forgive us of our sins and purify us from all unrighteousness." We are called to serve those caught in sin by being the first representative of this truth to those we love.

Serve Those with Burdens

We are also free to serve by carrying the burdens of those around us. If there is a word that describes many people in our society, even within the church, it is the word "burdened." Parents with newborn children are exhausted from rocking their kids all night and working all day. Business owners are stressed with the pressures of paying employees and making a profit. People in most churches need money for food, some sort of car repair, or help with a major house project. Some are physically frazzled from taking care of an aged parent. Others face the daily task of caring for a handicapped child. Couples have bills to pay and work to do. Students have the pressure of making the grade and excelling in sports, all while they hold down a part-time job. This is not to mention those who carry emotional insecurities, spiritual temptations, and past failures around with them like a knapsack thrown over their backs. Who will help all these people if not those who are a part of the same Body?

Many times, at the end of our small group time, I'll ask the simple question, "Does anyone have any practical needs we can meet?" This is our small group's practice to ensure we are helping each other with life. This simple question has led to paint parties, preparing a baby nursery, cleaning a basement, moving (a most popular small group activity), helping with minor car repair, giving parental advice, and supplying money for tomorrow's school lunch. All these and many others are burdens we are called to help one another bear. If Christians don't help one another, what kind of freedom is that?

The apostle points out in verse two that when we serve each other like this we fulfill the law of Christ. Jesus came to earth and took on the form of a servant (see Phil 2:7) even to the point of washing his disciples' feet. By his servanthood we have been set free so that we can serve others. This service, in turn, brings freedom to those we help. Our service takes away part of the bondage that often accompanies the above-mentioned worries.

Serve Authentically

There is a very interesting word in verse four of our study. It is the word "test." Have you ever paid for something at a convenience store or fast food place with a twenty dollar bill only to have the cashier take the money and hold it up to the light? She is looking for signs of counterfeit. Most workers who handle lots of cash have been trained to look for money that is not real. They know that real twenty dollar bills have specific markings and colors to indicate their authenticity. The word translated as "test" here was a word from the Galatian marketplaces. It too was a word associated with testing the authenticity of the money as it changed hands. Who knew that even Galatia had counterfeiters?

The point for serving is this: serve others in a sincere and authentic way. Authentic serving has to do with carrying your own load (6:5). Each of us is given specific abilities and gifts as designed by the Father. We are called to use those to serve others. But we are not called to help in ways beyond our capability. I have been called to preach. I love preaching. I'm comfortable preaching. It is a passion for me. In my ministry, I also help all kinds of people through all kinds of problems, but there are some things I just can't help with. If you need your car fixed, I'm the wrong guy. To volunteer my services as a mechanic wouldn't be serving at all. In fact, it would actually hurt the situation. If someone asks me to help in an area I sincerely can't help in, it is most honest for me to decline and try to reference them to someone who can help. This is authentic serving.

In turn, authenticity keeps me from comparing my service to others. Many times Christians make the mistake of thinking that some service opportunities are more important than others. Some are more visible, but none are more important. Each time we serve, we are serving Christ and that makes it vital. The point is not to compare. We shouldn't be bragging or calling attention to the service that we do; nor should we feel our service to be insignificant or less important than the service of others. When we serve, we should simply hold up our motives to the light to see if they are authentic offerings of freedom on God's behalf. If we pass this test, serving others brings freedom to us and them.

> **Christians make the mistake of thinking that some service opportunities are more important.**

Serve by Sowing

The final expectation of serving is that we serve as a spiritual farmer. Every day is filled with action. The apostle says that each of those actions is either seed sown for destruction or for eternal life. If we serve ourselves by gratifying our personal desires and pleasures, we will reap destruction. However, if we take every opportunity to serve others, we are in line with the Spirit's desires and we are growing a heavenly crop. There are not many things that you and I can do that have eternal implications. Much of the office work, housework, and schoolwork we spend our lives on will not mean one thing on the other side of eternity. Serving, on the other hand, will allow us to reap an eternal reward. God can't be mocked. We may think he doesn't see our unwillingness to help others. We may assume he can't tell we are using our freedom to indulge ourselves. But he sees and he knows. When we serve, he causes that service to grow into an eternal freedom for both the servant and the served.

God has set us free so that we can authentically help one another through sin and with our burdens, planting eternal seeds in the process. Our teaching today tells us to look for every chance to serve others in this way especially toward those with whom we worship (see 6:10). You are free to serve. Enjoy! ⊞

---

[1] Vergilius Ferm, *Classics of Prostestantism* (New York: Philosophical Library, 1959) 41.

Living Free

1. Who in your church has a need? How can you help?

2. Who in your small group has a need? How can you help?

3. Who in your work or social setting has a need? How can you help?

4. What is the most authentic way for you to serve? What are you doing right now to serve in your passion area?

5. Adopt a monthly service project as a small group.

6. Read John 13:1-17 and have a foot-washing service with your small group. As you take turns washing one another's feet, pray that God will help you to have a servant's heart.

Memory Verse
Gal 6:9-10

Let us not become weary in doing good, for at the proper time we will reap a harvest if we do not give up. [10]Therefore, as we have opportunity, let us do good to all people, especially to those who belong to the family of believers.

CHAPTER ELEVEN

FREEDOM'S SYMBOL

GALATIANS 6:11-18

THIS IS THE LAST CHAPTER AND I REALLY WANT TO GET YOUR ATTENTION! AS WE FINISH THIS BOOK ON FREEDOM I WANT TO DRAW YOUR HEART TO ITS MOST IMPORTANT SYMBOL. THE APOSTLE CLOSED HIS LETTER TO THESE GALATIAN CHRISTIANS IN THE SAME WAY. HIS DESIRE WAS TO DIRECT THEIR ATTENTION BACK TO FREEDOM'S MOST ENDURING CHRISTIAN SYMBOL—THE CROSS. HE USED LARGE LETTERS TO DO SO.

Most teachers in the first century used a stenographer or scribe (called an amanuensis) to write while they dictated the content of letters and teachings. The apostle Paul was no different. In all likelihood, much of the New Testament was spoken by the apostle but handwritten by someone else. These professional writers were people who took great pride in writing style and the precise formation of the letters. Apparently Paul had dictated Galatians 1:1 through Galatians 6:10, but then for dramatic effect, he asks for the writer's pen, dips it into the ink, and writes, "See what large letters I use as I write to you with my own hand!" The visual difference between the stenographer's penmanship and the apostle's would have drawn attention to the words which followed.

Why did the apostle write with large letters? We know he was well educated, but that doesn't mean his writing was legible (most doctors and scholars are known for poor penmanship). Perhaps his letters were large because of his inability to write well. Some believe that his hands had been damaged from his occupation as a tent-maker and as a result of his multiple beatings and stonings. This would make writing difficult. The most popular theory about the large letters was that Paul's thorn in the flesh mentioned in 2 Corinthians 12:7 was some sort of eye malady. This is supported from a passage in this letter as well (see Gal 4:15).

All of these ideas may have some truth to them, but I believe that, as the apostle neared the end of the letter, he wanted to get his readers' attention to wrap up his freedom message. He wanted them to know that the cross was the whole point, and he wanted them to know he was intimately connected to it. So he wrote about the cross with big letters and in his own handwriting. Let's examine what he wrote.

Read Galatians 6:11-18 together as a group.

In our culture the cross is a familiar symbol. You can see crosses formed from gold and silver hanging from the necks of rap stars, sports stars, and movie stars. The cross is a design for tattoos, earrings, and artwork. Crosses adorn the tops of many church steeples as well as their interior design. There are Celtic crosses, Lutheran crosses, Catholic crosses, and Christian crosses. You don't have to look far to find a cross. But something tells me that the apostle wasn't interested in the cross as a fashion statement. To him it was the focal point of his life, his ministry, and his freedom. In the closing comments of this letter there are three distinct challenges he gives the believer concerning the cross.

> You don't have to look far to find a cross.

Don't Avoid the Cross

At the end of this defense of freedom the apostle exposes the motivation that truly drives his opponents. "The only reason they do this is to avoid being persecuted for the cross of Christ" (6:12). The people who were pushing adherence to the Mosaic Law and the practice of circumcision were doing so only because they didn't want to align themselves with the cross of Jesus. What appears to be religious zeal is in fact cowardice. The law and the rituals that accompany them call for an amount of sacrifice and hard work, but the cross asks for your life. There is no way to come to a freedom relationship with Jesus without the cross. Jesus himself set this standard during his ministry when he said, "Anyone who does not carry his cross and follow me cannot be my disciple" (Luke 14:27).

Paul didn't avoid the cross. It was the focal point of his message, and he knew it

> There is no way to come to a freedom relationship with Jesus without the cross.

was going to get him in trouble just about every time. Imagine the emotional roller coaster that Paul endured every time he entered a new city. He was dedicated to preaching the cross (a well-known instrument of execution) in direct opposition to the idolatry that was present in most locations. Yet he knew that this message of the cross would in all likelihood bring him some form of persecution. Imagine preachers living in terror every Sunday morning, concerned that their audience may beat them or stone them because of the message. In spite of this constant pressure and physical pain, Paul (and many other first-century followers) continued to preach.

Isn't it interesting that in a culture where believers are not persecuted for what they say about the cross, many of us still avoid it? Oh sure, we'll put an Ichthus (the popular fish which was an early symbol of Christianity) on our car and we'll proudly wear a WWJD bracelet. It has even become vogue among many young believers to get cross, Ichthus, and crown of thorn tattoos. As a symbol we don't shy away from the cross, but that doesn't necessarily mean we aren't avoiding it. In this culture everyone wears a cross, but that doesn't mean they are followers of the Savior who died there. It is easier to wear the cross than to bear the cross.

> **It is easier to wear the cross than to bear the cross.**

How does the 21st-century Christian embrace the cross like our first-century brothers and sisters? We do so by embracing the totality of its message in such a way that it sets us apart. This is subtle but, I believe, important. When we work with someone for years and they don't know we are Christian, is that because we are avoiding the cross? When the topic of religion or God comes up in our social gatherings, do we offer insight about freedom found in the cross, or are we surprisingly quiet? When someone makes mention of our cross tattoo or Ichthus bumper sticker, do we brush it off as something we just thought was cool, or do we share that our lives are dependent on this symbol? Many times I'm afraid our silence and timidity when it comes to the cross are nothing more than avoiding the embarrassment of being labeled as a radical or "Bible thumper." There is no way to freedom aside from embracing the cross and the persecution that necessarily follows.

Take Pride in the Cross

In verses 13 and 14 of this letter the apostle penned the word "boast." This is a pride word, a word that signifies bragging about some advantage, ability, or superiority over another. We brag about athletic accomplishments, academic achievements, personal success, professional promotions, and financial or material acquisitions. But there are some things we don't brag about. Most in our society don't brag about weaknesses, failures, disappointments, or setbacks. It just doesn't make sense to brag about something that proves your weakness. Yet the apostle used the word "boast" to contrast the two messages the Galatians were hearing.

Those opposed to the freedom message were boastful for sure, but they bragged about the flesh. I don't know how those who were preaching circumcision measured their success, but apparently they did in part by counting the number of people who were circumcised. Did they have an attendance chart with attendance, offering total, and circumcisions? Probably not, but for them, success was measured by how many they convinced that the law was still in effect, and the most outward reflection of that was the permanence of circumcision. Contrary to their message, the apostle teaches that circumcision is nothing; he preaches something else that counts for so much more.

That's why he boasted in the cross of Jesus. Paul could've bragged about his heritage as it pertained to the law and the Jewish faith. In Philippians 3:4-7, he outlines his religious credentials. He was young, zealous, from the right family, and a strict follower of the law, but he died to all of that for the sake of Christ. While the Judaizers bragged about the outward change of circumcision, the apostle boasted in the cross because it brought about an internal, spiritual change. Read Galatians 6:15 again: "Neither circumcision nor uncircumcision means anything; what counts is a new creation." The cross made the apostle a new creation by setting him free, literally changing him from the slave that he was into the free man he had become in Christ.

When we consider what each of us has been and what God has done in our lives to make us who we have become, we find something to brag about. Even though they have been changed by God's grace, Christians sometimes have a tendency to brag about their gifts or accomplishments. These words from Galatians teach us that boasting is something we should never do unless we brag about the radical life transformation and the freedom that we have found in the cross. We are called not to brag about what we are, but about what we are becoming in Christ.

> We brag not about what we are, but about what we are becoming in Christ.

Let the Cross Mark Your Life

Finally the apostle comes to the last few strokes of this letter on freedom, and he finishes with a flair. There is an interesting word in verse seventeen that is familiar to us, but had cultural meaning to his Galatian audience. The word that is translated as "marks" is the Greek word "stigmata." In the first century this was the word used to describe the mark put on a slave to designate ownership. It could be something like a tattoo or branding that marked the slave for a certain master. And in this verse, the apostle aligns himself with slavery to the cross by saying he bears the marks of Jesus in his body.

Again there is a bit of irony here, for the major component of the opposition's argument was circumcision. Of course, circumcision, being the flesh altering surgery that it was, also left an indelible mark on the male who was committed to following the Jewish faith. If you were to ask a Jewish male to show proof of his faith in God, it would not be out of line for him to show his mark. The fact that he was circumcised was the mark of his enslavement to the law. It was his "stigmata." While there was an amount of pain and sacrifice that accompanied a circumcision, the apostle bore in his body more impressive marks.

The marks of Jesus were those mentioned by the apostle Thomas. He said in John 20:25, "Unless I see the nail marks (stigmata) in his hands and put my finger where the nails were, and put my hand into his side, I will not believe it." The marks that Jesus bore on his body were two nail holes in his hands, two in his feet, and the piercing in his side. Of course, he also had marks from the cruel scourging he received before the cross, and the crown of thorns would have scarred his brow. So what was Paul saying when he claimed to bear in his body the marks of Jesus?

More than likely he was not referring to literal crucifixion scars. He was saying in a symbolic way that the cross had left marks on his body. We know that Paul lists several instances of persecution in 2 Corinthians 11:23ff. He no doubt had several scars as a result of his preaching about the cross. Perhaps he had several scars on his head and face where stones thrown from overzealous Jews met their mark. Having endured several scourgings, it is a safe assumption that his back would be striped with scars. Some debris or timber from the shipwreck may have cut him on the arm or leg as he plunged into the sea. Perhaps as he looked at the hand he was writing with, he noticed the scars and realized that the cross has marked his body. If you were to ask Paul for proof of his attachment to Christ and the cross, he would simply show you the scars and tell you the stories that went with each.

Which leads me to ask this question: "How has the cross marked us?" If you are like me, you've got scars. I have one on my knee from my childhood from a protruding nail on a slide. Maybe you can identify each scar and the occasion for each. But how many of us have been scarred because of the cross? While most of us may never get a physical scar in the line of Christian duty, it is important that we maintain the right attitude that goes with carrying the cross. It is the same attitude as that of the apostle. We allow the world to be crucified to us and us to the world. The cross should be leaving a mark on the way we live our lives, the way we talk, the dreams we have, the thoughts we have, and the future we hope for. The cross is an instrument of death. There

How has the cross marked us? is no way to endure the cross without receiving some marks. These marks indicate our slavery to our Lord who died there, and they are proof of our dedication to its cause.

In the year 1224 the famous ascetic, Francis of Assisi, made his way into the Mountains of Alverna in his Italian homeland. After an extended period of fasting and prayer and taking in the natural surroundings, he reappeared with "stigmata." He bore on his body the five marks of Jesus in his hands, feet, and side. People throughout the ages have turned this into legend and consider it to be a special revelation. I don't know exactly what happened in that mountain, but I do know that St. Francis illustrates what the cross must do in each of our spiritual lives.

THE GRACE OF OUR LORD JESUS CHRIST BE WITH YOUR SPIRIT, BROTHERS. AMEN. FREEDOM! 3:18

Living Free

1. When is it most tempting to avoid the cross by denying and downplaying your faith and commitment to Christ?

2. What kinds of things that you have, have done, or can do, would most tempt you to boast? Are they really worth boasting about in the big picture of life?

3. Take a minute to talk about the scars (physical and emotional) that you have received in life. How do they compare with the sacrs of Jesus and Paul?

4. What mark has the cross left on your life? Spiritually? Emotionally? Physically? Share these scars with your group as well.

Memory Verse Gal 6:14

May I never boast except in the cross of our Lord Jesus Christ, through which the world has been crucified to me, and I to the world.

Strength for the Journey
Hebrews
Jeff Snell
108 pages, softcover, G316-917-4, $6.99

HeartSpring Publishing
1-800-289-3300 • www.heartspringpublishing.com

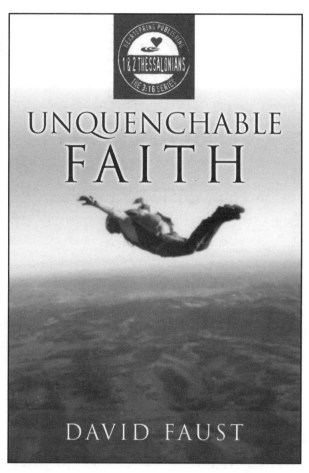

Unquenchable Faith
1 & 2 Thessalonians
David Faust
137 pages, softcover, G316-492-X, $7.49

HeartSpring Publishing
1-800-289-3300 • www.heartspringpublishing.com

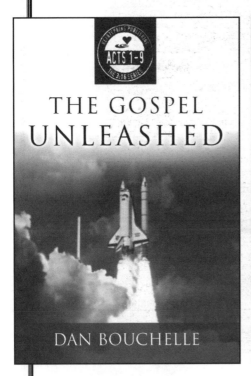
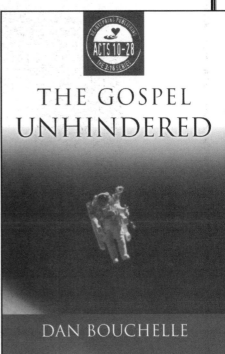

GALATIANS MEMORY VERSES

Cut on dotted line

Galatians 1:11-12

11 I want you to know, brothers, that the gospel I preached is not something that man made up. 12 I did not receive it from any man, nor was I taught it; rather, I received it by revelation from Jesus Christ.

Galatians 2:7-8

7 On the contrary, they saw that I had been entrusted with the task of preaching the gospel to the Gentiles, just as Peter had been to the Jews. 8 For God, who was at work in the ministry of Peter as an apostle to the Jews, was also at work in my ministry as an apostle to the Gentiles.

Galatians 2:20

20 I have been crucified with Christ and I no longer live, but Christ lives in me. The life I live in the body, I live by faith in the Son of God, who loved me and gave himself for me.

Galatians 3:6

6 Consider Abraham: "He believed God, and it was credited to him as righteousness."

Galatians 3:24-25

24 So the law was put in charge to lead us to Christ that we might be justified by faith. 25 Now that faith has come, we are no longer under the supervision of the law.

Galatians 3:26-27

26 You are all sons of God through faith in Christ Jesus, 27 for all of you who were baptized into Christ have clothed yourselves with Christ.

Galatians 4:8-9

8 Formerly, when you did not know God, you were slaves to those who by nature are not gods. 9 But now that you know God—or rather are known by God—how is it that you are turning back to those weak and miserable principles? Do you wish to be enslaved by them all over again?

Galatians 5:6

6 For in Christ Jesus neither circumcision nor uncircumcision has any value. The only thing that counts is faith expressing itself through love.

Galatians 5:22-23

22 But the fruit of the Spirit is love, joy, peace, patience, kindness, goodness, faithfulness, 23 gentleness and self-control. Against such things there is no law.

Galatians 6:9-10

9 Let us not become weary in doing good, for at the proper time we will reap a harvest if we do not give up. 10 Therefore, as we have opportunity, let us do good to all people, especially to those who belong to the family of believers.

Galatians 6:14

14 May I never boast except in the cross of our Lord Jesus Christ, through which the world has been crucified to me, and I to the world.

HEART
SPRING